STUDIA JUDAICA

1

THE FORM AND FUNCTION
OF
PROVERBS IN ANCIENT ISRAEL

by

JOHN MARK THOMPSON

Kalamazoo College

1974

MOUTON

THE HAGUE · PARIS

LIBRARY OF CONGRESS CATALOG CARD NUMBER: 72-94508

Printed in The Netherlands

ACKNOWLEDGMENTS

I want here to express my sincere appreciation to my mentors, whose counsel and encouragement were so very helpful in my original work on this subject: Dr. J. Philip Hyatt, whose recent death is a considerable loss to the world of biblical research, Dr. Lou H. Silberman and Dr. Walter Harrelson. I also thank my wife, who has contributed her considerable typing skill to this enterprise, and who has been faithfully supportive in my work.

Kalamazoo College   John Mark Thompson

CREDITS

PREFACE

THE PROBLEM

Among the books of the Old Testament which have suffered loss of prestige over the years, perhaps Proverbs has suffered most. The prophets are seen as speaking relevantly to our time as well as to their own; the historical themes of election and covenant are highly valued as keystones to the understanding of biblical theology; even the book of Esther can be commended as a good story; and the Song of Songs, de-allegorized at last, has won a certain esteem as a reflection of the Hebrew's enjoyment of sex. But Proverbs, alas, remains either un-noticed or scorned, "a potpourri of sayings and short poems, generally mediocre as literature, tedious as ethics, banal as religion".[1]

Such ignominy has not always been Proverbs' portion, or certainly it never could have won its place among the sacred scriptures of Judaism and Christianity. Nor could it have gained the popularity it has continued to enjoy until comparatively recent years. Martin Luther held the work in high esteem. Ruskin, who was compelled by his mother to memorize four chapters from the book, later claimed them to be "the most precious and on the whole essential part of all my education".[2] John Paterson has written that it "has always been the favorite book of Scotsmen: probably no other book of the Bible has had a more lasting influence on the character of that people".[3] He

1   Norman K. Gottwald, *A Light to the Nations* (New York: Harper & Brothers, 1959), p. 472.
2   William A.L. Elmslie, *Studies in Life from Jewish Proverbs* (London: James Clark & Co., 1917), p. 30.
3   John Paterson, *The Book That is Alive* (New York: Charles Scribner's Sons, 1954), p. 72.

even suggests that Proverbs played a significant role in the establishment of the British Empire.[4]

With Luther now as popular as ever in Protestant circles, and with
no notable increase in the number of Anglophobes within the ranks of
biblical scholars, it does seem that someone ought to search out the
reasons for Proverbs' sad fate and endeavor to establish what it is that
led to its continued influence through the centuries.

It is the conviction of the writer that, properly understood, Proverbs well deserves both its place within the Canon and the high
regard which it formerly received. And it is the defense of this conviction which constitutes the burden of our study.

The major research for this book was done during the early sixties,
a time when scholars were just beginning to re-examine carefully the
Wisdom heritage of Israel. My study was submitted to Vanderbilt
University in the form of a Ph. D. dissertation in 1965; and now, some
eight years later, I still find myself in essential agreement with what I
wrote then.

Since 1965, of course, Wisdom's cry has become increasingly loud
in the academic arena; and the search for Wisdom's influence throughout the Bible has become the passion of more than one or two
scholars. In these pages I, too, see Wisdom's far reaching influence
through the pages of the Old Testament. Yet I must express appreciation for the critical observations and admonitions of J.L. Crenshaw
and Roland E. Murphy as they have viewed the contributions and
excesses of this new research.[5]

Among the scholars who have published important works during
the past few years, two have shared my view that the origins of
Israel's apodictic law are to be found in Wisdom: Erhard Gerstenberger and W. Richter.[6] Their works are rather more precisely focused

---

4   *Ibid.*

5   J.L. Crenshaw, "Method in Determining Wisdom Influence Upon 'Historical'
Literature", *Journal of Biblical Literature*, Vol. LXXXVIII (June, 1969), pp.
129-42; Roland E. Murphy, "Assumptions and Problems in Old Testament Wisdom Research", *Catholic Biblical Quarterly*, Vol. XXIX (July, 1967), pp.
101-12; See also J.L. Crenshaw, "The Influence of the Wise Upon Amos; the
Doxologies of Amos and Job 5:9-16, 9:5-10", *Zeitschrift für die alttestamentliche Wissenschaft*, Vol. LXXIX (1967), pp. 42-52.

6   Erhard Gerstenberger, "Covenant and Commandment", *Journal of Biblical
Literature*, Vol. LXXXIV (March, 1965), pp. 38-51; and *Wesen und Herkunft*

than my somewhat broad treatment, and center their attention upon
the form and function of the *Mahnwort*, which they see as being
antecedent to the prohibitive apodictic legal injunction. While they
see the line of development as proceding from Israel primarily (from
tribal schools, according to Richter; from ancient clan fathers, according to Gerstenberger), my own work points more in the direction of
Israelite court schools, greatly influenced by Egyptian Wisdom.

It isn't our intent here to deal precisely with all the various types of
proverb or saying that can be found in the Old Testament: *Aussage-
wort, Mahnwort*, etc., but to focus attention upon the esthetic dimension. And so it is much more appropriate for our purposes that we
understand that the general character of proverbs is frequently poetic
than that it may be classified into a number of distinct and identifiable types. For more detailed classification the reader is referred to
the standard Old Testament introductions and the more recent works
on biblical proverbs, especially those of R.B.Y. Scott and Hans-Jürgen
Hermisson.[7]

METHOD

We shall begin our study by noting briefly some of the factors which
would seem to be responsible for the recent eclipse of Proverbs. It will
be noted, among other things, that we no longer appreciate the form
of our biblical proverbs, that we fail to perceive their importance
within the context of Hebrew life and faith, and that we are captive to
the Hebrew skeptic's caveat vis à vis much proverbial wisdom.

Since these would seem to be serious problems, we shall devote the

---

des 'Apodiktischen Rechts' (=*Wissenschaftliche Monographien zum Alten und
Neuen Testament*, Vol. XX) (Neukirchen-Vluyn: Neukirchen Verlag, 1965); W.
Richter, *Recht und Ethos* (=*Studien zum Alten und Neuen Testament*, Vol XV)
(München: Kösel-Verlag, 1966).

7 R.B.Y. Scott, *Proverbs, Ecclesiastes* (=*The Anchor Bible*, Vol. XVIII)
(Garden City, New York: Doubleday & Company, Inc., 1965); Hans-Jürgen
Hermisson, *Studien zur Israelitischen Spruchweisheit* (=*Monographien zum Alten und Neuen Testament*, Vol. XXVIII) (Neukirchen-Vluyn: Neukirchener Verlag, 1968).

major portion of the work to dealing with them. In the course of our inquiry we shall first of all examine proverbs in general: their universal features and the role they play in the life of man. Secondly, we shall look at the proverbs of the ancient Near East and investigate their role in Egyptian, Babylonian and Canaanite culture. Next we shall, by looking at Hebrew proverbs in relation to the proverb form in general, to the proverbs of surrounding civilizations and to other elements of Hebraic culture, attempt to assess their importance in Hebrew life and thought. And finally we shall deal with the skeptical element in ancient Hebrew Wisdom, relating it to the skepticism of ancient wisdom in general and to the optimistic tenor of Israel's proverbs, with which it seems to be so frequently at odds.

TABLE OF CONTENTS

INTRODUCTION

That the book of Proverbs no longer claims the high favor once accorded it hardly needs demonstration. The book receives scant attention in Bible textbooks and scholarly literature. What notice it does receive may be indicated solely by its presence in the Canon. And the comments upon it can be less than complimentary.

Six reasons may be suggested for this decline in popularity, some reflecting mostly a shift in values which has occurred in relatively recent times, others reflecting our cultural distance from the ancient Hebrews. Three of them call for further investigation.

The first reason why this book no longer speaks to us as it did to our ancestors is that proverbs in general no longer enjoy the popularity which was once theirs.[1] To be sure, there will always be some who find the aphorism attractive; as recently as 1962 the Secretary of the Paroemiological Society published an impressive collection of proverbs, in part contributed by the diplomats of the United Nations and in part culled by the editor from his private 4,000 volume library on the subject.[2] But paroemiologists are a rare breed, and the fact remains that proverbs are no longer in vogue.

Back in the tenth century they were used by clerks in teaching their novices the intricacies of Latin grammar; throughout the Middle Ages they were a necessary ingredient of polished rhetoric; and

---

[1] Yet Fritsch notes that the book is still popular on the mission field: "Its attractive rhythmical form, its humor, and the ease with which it is understood seem to account for its acceptability to young Christian converts in non-Christian lands". Charles T. Fritsch, "The Gospel in the Book of Proverbs", *Theology Today*, Vol. VII (April, 1950), p. 170.

[2] V.S.M. de Guinzbourg (ed.), *Wit and Wisdom of the United Nations* (New York: V.S.M. de Guinzbourg, 1961).

by the beginning of Elizabeth's reign every one — scholars, wits, courtiers, writers, the queen herself — spoke and wrote in proverbs, even
invented them. They welcomed them for their common sense, or
because of the 'sweet relished phrases' that struck the wide-open eyes
and ears of the time with a delicious novelty; and they used them
because writing was still under the influence of the rhetoricians.[3]

But times change, and literary conventions along with them; and by
the year 1741 Lord Chesterfield could write to his son that "a man of
fashion never has recourse to proverbs and vulgar aphorisms".[4] They
are, he says, "so many proofs of having kept bad and low company".[5]
Still, Americans of that day continued to have their characters formed,
in part at least, by the power of the proverb. The voice of Poor Richard
carried across the land, telling one and all to

> Get what you can, and what you get hold;
> 'Tis the stone that will turn all your lead into gold.[6]

But today, with the exception of an occasional recollection or as an
adornment to some cheap commercial calendar, the noble proverb has
been laid to rest alongside Poor Richard.

It is not our task here to plumb the mysteries of cultural change or
fathom the reasons for shifting tastes, but only to indicate that with
the passing of the popular proverb from fashion, it is little wonder
that our canonical collection shared its oblivion.

A second reason is perhaps a part of the first, but still deserves
separate notice. The choice phrase, displaying that perfect aptness and
originality of the good proverb, so lends itself to continuous repetition that it soon becomes trite. For example, Franklin Roosevelt's
"The only thing we have to fear is fear itself" was once a word of
encouragement; it became a popular proverb. But today one can
scarcely quote it without apology, even when it fits the situation. As

---

3 Janet E. Heseltine, "Introduction", *The Oxford Dictionary of English
Proverbs*, ed. George William Smith (Oxford: The Clarendon Press, 1936), p.
xiv.
4 *Ibid.*
5 *Ibid.*
6 Benjamin Franklin, "Poor Richard's Almanac and Other Papers", *The
Autobiography of Benjamin Franklin, Poor Richard's Almanac, and Other Papers* (*The Home Library*) (New York: A.L. Burt, n.d.), p. 230.

Elmslie has put it, "Every effort to indicate the genius of proverbs is attended by the disadvantage of verbal familiarity; and, of course, it is the finest sayings that suffer most."[7] As one needs to remind oneself that the trite melody of a Tschaikovsky symphony wasn't trite when it was first heard, so one needs to remember that the banality of the proverb may testify more to its universal appeal than to any intrinsic defect.

As for our canonical proverbs in particular, they fail to reach us, it would seem, for still a third reason: they are jumbled together willy-nilly into collections. Granted that much of the Bible lacks the kind of organization we might like to impose upon it, the phenomenon of a plethora of distichs, many having little or nothing in common with what precedes or what follows, is peculiar to this book, particularly to chapters 10-29.

"To read consecutively through a series of these self-contained units is to impose an intolerable strain on the mind. The imagination becomes jaded, the memory dazed by the march of too swiftly changing images. The disconnected thoughts efface one another, leaving behind them only a blurred confusion.[8]

A fourth barrier to our understanding, and one which will be discussed further, is a lack of appreciation of the form of the biblical proverb. The word 'appreciation' is used deliberately here rather than 'comprehension' or 'understanding' or some comparable cognitive term, since we certainly do know a good deal about the external structure of this genre of literature. But just as one may be able to scan a poem intelligently without being grasped by its power, so we may term a proverb 'antithetic ternary' and yet be totally unmoved by it.

It would be naïve to assume, of course, that a study of this type could somehow engender a kind of 'esthetic awareness' of the proverb's power on the part of the reader. But perhaps it is not too immodest to hope that a discussion of the relationship of the proverb's form to its content, and of the psychological result of this

---

7 Elmslie, *op. cit.*, p. 15.

8 Elmslie, *op. cit.*, p. 16; See also Berend Gemser, *Sprüche Salomos* (Tübingen: J.C.B. Mohr, 1937), p. 7.

relationship, may enhance our appreciation of this ancient type of expression.

A fifth problem which presents itself is our failure to understand the function of the proverb in ancient Israel. How did this type of expression fit in with other elements of Hebrew culture? How basic a part of this culture was it? In what ways was it related to the thinking of the prophets or the priests? All too frequently Proverbs — and indeed the wisdom literature generally — is treated as a foreign and intrusive element in Hebrew life and thought. We shall, in our final chapters, attempt to establish some basic connections between proverb lore and certain other important elements of Israel's culture.

A sixth and final difficulty which we encounter is the fact that the high confidence in human reason and the happy doctrine of rewards and punishments which most of Israel's proverbs seem to embrace cannot withstand either the telling thrusts of the biblical skeptics, Job and Koheleth, or of our own personal experience. And therefore we shall attempt to understand, within the context of ancient Near Eastern and Hebrew culture, the proper relationship between the so-called 'prudential wisdom' and its more skeptical counterpart.

1. PROVERBS IN GENERAL

Before discussing the proverbs in the ancient Near East and of Israel, it is necessary to understand something of the proverb in general. What is it? How may it differ from a simple declarative statement or question? With what does it deal? How does it originate? How is it preserved? Where is it found in the world?

It is the intent of this work to move from a general understanding, or extended definition, of the proverb to the particular biblical examples. We are interested in that form of expression which in Western Culture is called a 'proverb' or an 'aphorism' or a 'saying', rather than all that the ancient Hebrew meant by his term *mashal*. For him the term, besides its narrower meaning, embraced all that we might designate as parables, allegories, oracles of blessing and cursing, taunts, poems, essays,[1] and perhaps even acts of magic.[2]

DEFINITION

If we are to define what we mean by the term 'proverb', we must content ourselves with only a very general description. For even within the limits of our Western, Non-Hebrew understanding of the term,

---

[1] Aage Bentzen, *Introduction to the Old Testament*, Vol. II (Copenhagen: G.E.C. Gad, 1949), p . 167; Abraham Cohen, *Proverbs* (Hindhead, Surrey: Soncino Press, 1945), p. xii; Arthur J. Culler, *Creative Religious Literature* (New York: The Macmillan Company, 1930), p. 72; Charles T. Fritsch, "The Book of Proverbs, Introduction and Exegesis", *Interpreter's Bible*, Vol. IV, pp. 771-72; Harry Ranston, *The Old Testament Wisdom Books and Their Teaching* (London: Epworth Press, 1930), pp. 38-40.

[2] Allen Howard Godbey, "The Hebrew Mashal", *American Journal of Semitic Languages and Literatures*, Vol. XXXIX (1922/3), pp. 89-108.

one can identify widely differing types. Both with regard to content and to form the variations, even within a given culture and language, are many. And when one considers in addition the types that are peculiar to this or that culture or linguistic setting, then any attempt at precise definition becomes impossible. As Archer Taylor has written, "The definition of a proverb is too difficult to repay the undertaking; and should we fortunately combine in a single definition all the essential elements and give each the proper emphasis, we should not even then have a touchstone."[3]

Yet, in a very general way, one may attempt to say what the proverb is. While the frequently quoted words of Lord Russell, "The wisdom of many, the wit of one",[4] are somewhat brief, they do point to three very common features of proverbial lore: (1) an arresting and individually inspired form ("wit of one"), (2) a wide appeal and endorsement ("of many"), and (3) content which commends itself to the hearer as true ("wisdom").

Sometimes it would seem that uniqueness of form is almost entirely lacking, but the content has sufficient appeal to win a wide audience. For example, the familiar saying, "You can lead a horse to water but you can't make him drink" has little in its form which would appear to guarantee its survival; only the applicability of the content seems to be the sustaining factor. On the other hand, form may preserve a parable whose content is not otherwise capable of sustaining it. "He who laughs last laughs longest" might well not survive were it not for its striking assonance and alliteration. But take a proverb whose applicability is universal and whose form is compelling, and its survival seems assured. "Look before you leap" enjoins caution and displays alliteration; it is therefore doubly durable.

Beyond this expansion of Russell's dictum one might only add that the proverb is usually short, easy to remember and most frequently transmitted orally. We shall take up a more thorough discussion of

---

3 Archer Taylor, *The Proverb and an Index to the Proverb* (Hatboro, Pennsylvania: Folklore Associates; Copenhagen: Rosenkilde and Bagger, 1962), p. 3.

4 This is actually a misquotation; what Russell really seems to have said is this: "A Proverb is one man's wit and all men's wisdom". See Burton Stevenson, ed., *The Home Book of Quotations* (New York: Dodd, Mead, and Company, 1956), p. 1629.

form and function later, but for purposes of rough categorization we need elaborate no further here.

ORIGINS

How and when do particular proverbs originate? In most cases one simply cannot answer this question. Most proverbs begin as oral rather than written sayings, and so betray no clue by way of date of publication or author's signature. And even when proverbs are sometimes included in written works, such as was common in sixteenth century England,[5] they may have been current at the time and of unknown age.

Occasionally a written or clearly identifiable word does become proverbial, and so both its author and date can be fairly closely pinned down. Shakespeare's "to be or not to be" can be considered such a proverbial saying.[6] Or, to cite one contemporary example, Winston Churchill's World War Two tribute to the R.A.F. may well become a proverbial phrase applicable to other situations: "Never ... was so much owed to so few." Ordinarily, however, some unknown person, living in an unknown era, has, in a moment of creative insight, given eloquent expression to a universal fact of life or common experience, which has then been quoted with delight under similar circumstances from his time to our own.

To complicate the picture further, the proverb is commonly passed down orally from generation to generation; it is thereby subject to infinite change, variation and application. And such possibilities make hazardous any attempt at dating on the basis of language. Such means, however, may have some limited validity. "Many a little makes a mickle" could safely be ruled out of twentieth century America, even if it was not to be found in English letters.

Occasional proverbs can be dated by a clear historical reference, but these, too, are rare. When we speak of someone "meeting his Waterloo" there can be little doubt as to the general time of origin, although even here one can be certain only of the *terminus a quo*. Of similar origin are those sayings based upon stories, fables or myths.

---

5 Heseltine, *op. cit.*, p. xiv.
6 Taylor, *op. cit.*, p. 34.

Our Aesopian "sour grapes" or "dog in the manger" are cases in point. But they are no easier to deal with than those making historical allusions.

While it is customary to make a distinction, with regard to origin, between the 'folk proverb' or 'popular saying' and its more sophisticated counterpart which is the product of deliberately applied artistry, it is doubtful whether such a differentiation is universally valid. Granting that many a *bon mot* has a polished sound to it, it simply will not do to classify it in either category if we have no clues beyond the proverb itself. Proverbs, we may be sure, do not emerge full-blown out of the collective mouth of 'the people'. In every case someone, somewhere, said the thing for the first time; and one cannot establish without further evidence the author's degree of sophistication. The muse, like God, is no respecter of persons; and the proverb, like a baby, has but one mother. When the existence of a class of 'wise men' can be reasonably postulated, however, and when their interest in proverbs can be established, then the distinction between the *Volksprichwort* and the *Kunstsprichwort*, or *Weisheitspruch*, may perhaps more legitimately be made. Or when a number of proverbs exhibit a clearly stereotyped form, one may suspect the influence of a 'school'.

UNIVERSALITY

Proverbs have been found almost everywhere in the world and from almost every period in human history. We know ancient Sumerian proverbs found on tablets from the second millennium B.C.[7] The proverb-like precepts of the Egyptian sages also go back to the second millennium. And in our own day such comprehensive collections as those of de Guinzbourg[8] or Champion[9] testify to widespread acquaintance with the proverb form.

Anthropologists also tell of the use of proverbs by less civilized

---

[7] Samuel Noah Kramer, *From the Tablets of Sumer* (Indian Hills, Colorado: Falcon's Wing Press, 1956), p. 153.

[8] de Guinzbourg, *op. cit.*

[9] Selwyn Gurney Champion, *Racial Proverbs* (New York: The Macmillan Company, 1938).

peoples, particularly those of Africa. It is interesting to note, however, that proverbs are not entirely universal, since they are practically unknown among the native American populations, either by the highly civilized Mayas and Incas or by their more primitive cousins.[10] But with this exception, proverbs seem to have been used the world over, in the West and in the East, and in civilizations which have long since disappeared. It would perhaps not be going too far to say that the proverb is the most ancient and widespread of man's speech forms.

FORM

Although the form of proverbs may vary considerably within a given culture and among cultures, we may point to certain aspects of form which appear in European languages, and which will later be seen to characterize the proverbs of other civilizations.

The simple, declarative statement or question is common. Beyond this, however, we find the frequent use of rhyme, meter, repetition, alliteration, assonance, simile, and metaphor.

Rhyme and meter are frequent. Our "There's many a slip 'twixt the cup and the lip" is typical, as are the following examples:

Fille qui prend, son corps vend.[11]

Es ist nichts so fein gesponnen,
es kommt doch endlich an die Sonnen.[12]

Andeme yo caliente,
y riase la gente.[13]

Meter was considered to be so important for medieval Latin proverbs that one finds useless words introduced into leonine hexameters solely for their metrical functions.[14]

---

10   Alfred L. Kroeber, *Anthropology* (New York: Harcourt, Brace and Co., 1923), p. 544; Franz Boas, "Literature, Music, and Dance", *General Anthropology*, ed. Franz Boas (New York: D.C. Heath & Co., 1938), p. 598.
11   de Guinzbourg, *op. cit.,* p. 283.
12   *Op. cit.*, p. 211.
13   *Op. cit.*, p. 208.
14   Taylor, *op. cit.*, p. 152.

Repetition is also common:

> A penny saved is a penny earned.

> Hostium munera non munera.[15]

> Autant vaut bien battu que mal battu.[16]

Alliteration characterized many proverbs, and seems to have been particularly popular in early Germanic verse:[17]

> He who hesitates is lost.

> Look before you leap.

> Wer fliegen will, muss einen Fittich haben.[18]

Assonance is frequently seen:

> A stitch in time saves nine.

> Many a little makes a mickle.

Similes occur occasionally:

> As hungry as a bear.

> A true friend should be like a privy, open in necessity.[19]

> Wie die Alten sungen,
> So switschern die Jungen.[20]

Metaphor is, of course, exceedingly frequent in the proverbs of many peoples:

---

15 de Guinzbourg, *op. cit.*, p. 283.
16 *Op. cit.*, p. 276.
17 Taylor, *op. cit.*, p. 137.
18 Edmund P. Kremer, *German Proverbs* (Stanford: Stanford University Press, 1955), p. 30.
19 de Guinzbourg, *op. cit.*, p. 48.
20 Kremer, *op. cit.*, p. 4.

You can't teach an old dog new tricks.

You can lead a horse to water, but you can't make him drink.

Non fiu mai si gran leone, che non havesse bisogno d'un sorsio.[21]

Zwei, Hund' an einen Bein
kommen selten uberein.[22]

The metaphorical proverb is abundantly present in African proverb lore. These Ba-ila examples are typical:

The prodigal cow threw away her own tail.[23]

It is the prudent hyena that lives long.[24]

A river that would not be straightened has bends in it (i.e. you lie on the bed you make).[25]

There would be little value in discussing proverbs on the basis of their use of this or that particular form, but the fact that these are typical forms of poetry is of especial significance. It does not mean that we can simply classify some proverbs as a kind of poetry, and let it go at that; for even the more 'poetic' proverb is still a proverb *sui generis*. But it may be suggested that the power of the proverb over the minds of men is closely akin to that of the poem, and that it frequently possesses this power by virtue of its use of poetic device. Furthermore, as we shall see, the basic forms of the canonical book of Proverbs and those of Hebrew poetry in general are the same.

It is impossible to state exactly what it is that happens in the human mind when it perceives the 'truth' of a poem or of a 'poetic proverb', but that it happens few would deny. It is as though, within the depths of human consciousness, we perceived the proverb's content to be true, not because of logical demonstration or even just its

---

21   de Guinzbourg, *op. cit.*, p. 36.
22   *Op. cit.*, p. 39.
23   Paul Radin, *Primitive Man as Philosopher* (New York: Dover Publications, Inc., 1957), p. 153.
24   *Ibid.*
25   Radin, *op. cit.*, p. 155.

appeal to 'common sense', but by the way in which it says what it has to say. Somehow the wisdom of "Look before you leap" is 'truer' than "Be cautious before undertaking a new enterprise". "A penny saved is a penny earned" is more convincing than the simple admonition "Be thrifty".

The commonplace truism, given an eloquent form, hits us almost as a fresh insight. Pearsal Smith has made this point in a particularly grandiloquent way:

To polish commonplaces and give them a new lustre; to express in a few words the obvious principle of conduct, and to give to clear thoughts an even clearer expression; to illuminate dimmer expressions and bring their faint rays to a focus; to delve beneath the surface of consciousness to new veins of precious ore, to name and discover and bring to light latent unnamed experience, and finally to embody the central truths of life in the breadth and terseness of memorable phrases — all these are the opportunities of the aphorist; and to take advantage of these opportunities, he must be a thinker, an accurate observer, a profound moralist, a psychologist, and an artist as well.[26]

It would seem that in Smith's thinking the proverb has much the same function as a poem: to lift up the commonplace in such an effective way that it is seen in a new and clearer light. To be sure, the proverb frequently deals with some principle of conduct and has a moral intent, while a good poet will generally eschew homiletics; but admitting this, it may still be contended that the two forms have much in common.

Perhaps we may put the matter differently and say that the proverb 'feels like' a poem. It has a similar 'emotional flavor', evokes a similar response, produces that satisfying 'Aha' of recognition which accompanies a moment of insight. Hans Sachs writes in his *The Creative Unconscious* words which, though applied there to poetry, might almost as fittingly refer to the good proverb:

We are facing here ... the phenomenon of the unlocking of closed gates by the influence of a work of art. The particular emotional situation which it permits us to experience for the first time has always been potentially in our possession. We feel convinced of it, we are sometimes even able to identify it afterwards. Yet, it was not

26 Quoted by Cohen, *op. cit.*, p. xiii.

within our unaided power to make it really our own, to possess it as a recognizable part of our personality, to distinguish it from other similar emotions, or to to call it back at will when our mood desired it. For all that we are indebted to the poem.[27]

In the same work Sachs, describing the experience of being 'under the spell of poetry', speaks of "the emergence of an emotional experience, which was hitherto only vaguely known, into full comprehension and intuitive understanding".[28]

We may say, then, that the proverb frequently, by use of common poetic devices, affects the hearer in very much the same way as the poem. It takes some simple fact of life or some everyday moral teaching and through its own particular form convinces the hearer. It is more than mere appeal to common experience in that it strikes emotional depths and calls forth not just intellectual assent, but inner conviction.

The fact that the proverb is generally a non-literary form is also particularly significant. And it (also like the poem) suffers when read silently. We Westerners are not, for the most part, sensitive to the spoken word, particularly the sententious word. We value books. The printed page, for some reason, speaks with exaggerated authority for us. One might venture to suggest that a footnote referring to an author's published work impresses us far more than one referring to an opinion by the same man put forth in private conversation. It is not our purpose here to attempt an explanation of this phenomenon, but one might guess that our continual bombardment by spoken words through radio and television has dulled our minds to their potential import. Many of the words bandied about in tawdry soap operas or silly commercials or other auditory trivia are, unfortunately, the same words which might be used in more significant ways. The spoken word has, in our time, been cheapened and emptied of its potential power. And the proverb, as an essentially oral form, has thereby suffered.

As an oral form, easily remembered and transmitted, the proverb quite naturally has had great importance among illiterate or preliterate peoples. Logically enough, when words cannot be read they are more

27 Hans Sachs, *The Creative Unconscious* (Cambridge, Mass.: Sci-Art Publishers, 1942), p. 202.
28 Sachs, *op. cit.*, p. 205.

highly valued when heard. The prominence of the story-teller among preliterate peoples is, of course, well known. The great popularity of proverbs among peoples of Africa is also frequently noted, and many of them have been collected and published.[29] An extract from the writings of C.M. Doke on the Lamba testifies to the currency of proverbs among these peoples:

Lamba proverbs seem to be without number. Since putting together the present collection I have gathered together another two hundred without any effort on my part; and a further number has been laid aside owing to lack of confirmation. Mulekelela, the Lamba story-teller, supplied me in the first place with more than half of these aphorisms: he has a wonderful mine of this lore, and one day reeled off as many as 250 at a single sitting. His work was ably seconded by Joshua Kamwendo, a native evangelist who was able to confirm and explain Mulekelela's proverbs and supply several hundred more.[30]

Elmslie, in noting the Arab's fondness for the spoken word and for proverbs in particular, cites the following passage from Doughty's *Arabia Deserta*:

These orientals study little else [than the art of conversation and narrative] as they sit all day idle in their male societies; they learn in this school of infinite human observation to speak to the heart of one another. His tales [referring to a Moorish rogue, Mohammed Aly] *seasoned with saws which are the wisdom of the unlearned,* we heard for more than two months; they were never-ending. He told them so lively to the eye that they could not be bettered, and part were of his own motley experience.[31]

Elmslie notes that among these people 'scriptural' language was common and for them neither pedantic nor 'religious'. Apparently the very sound of the words pouring forth gave delight in itself in addition

---

[29] See J.B. Danquah, *The Akan Doctrine of God* (London and Redhill: Lutterworth Press, 1944), pp. 189-97; Clement M. Doke, *Lamba Folk-Lore* (=*Memoirs of the American Folk-Lore Society*, Vol. XX) (New York: The American Folk-Lore Society, 1927); Kroeber, *op. cit.*, pp. 543-44; Edwin M. Loeb, "Kuanyama Ambo Folklore", *Anthropological Records*, Vol. XIII (1951), pp. 289-355; Radin, *op. cit.*, pp. 152-69.

[30] Doke, *op. cit.*, p. XVI.

[31] Elmslie, *op. cit.*, p. 56.

to what was conveyed by the specific content. Perhaps a clue to the kind of esthetic appreciation here suggested is given through the increased delight which many in our day take in hearing a poem read well. It takes on new life, we might say. It strikes us more profoundly through sound than it ever could through sight.

The medieval monks appear to have been well aware of this esthetic spiritual value of hearing – and indeed of speaking – the words of Holy Scripture. Jean Leclercq stresses the importance of this in his *The Love of Learning and the Desire for God*:

This repeated mastication of the divine words is sometimes described by use of the theme of spiritual nutrition. In this case the vocabulary is borrowed from eating, from digestion, and from the particular form of digestion belonging to the ruminants. For this reason, reading and meditation are sometimes described by the very expressive word *ruminatio*. For example, in praising a monk who prayed constantly, Peter the Venerable cried: "Without resting his mouth ruminated the sacred words". Of John of Gorze it was claimed that the murmur of his lips pronouncing the Psalms resembled the buzzing of a bee. To meditate is to attach oneself closely to the sentence being recited and weigh all its words in order to sound the depths of their full meaning. It means assimilating the content of the text by means of a kind of mastication which releases its full flavor. It means, as St. Augustine, St. Gregory, John of Fecamp and others say in an untranslatable expression to taste it with the *palatum cordis* or *in ore cordis*. [32]

To put the matter briefly, many proverbs from many places are characterized by their use of poetic devices, and convince the hearer in much the same way as poetry does. And also, like poetry, they must be spoken and heard in order to be fully appreciated.

FUNCTION

In discussing the function of proverbs we may distinguish between that function which is common to all proverbs everywhere and those specific uses to which they are frequently put. It will be suggested

---

[32] Jean Leclercq, *The Love of Learning and the Desire for God*, trans. Catherine Misrahi ("Mentor Omega Books"); (New York: New American Library, 1961), p. 78.

here that the common function of proverbs in general is that of bearing philosophical insight. And it will then be shown how these brief philosophical statements are variously employed.

If, by 'philosophy' we mean only the developed systems of Western thought, it cannot, of course, be maintained that proverb lore is philosophical. If, on the other hand, we mean the attempt by man to describe and understand the world in which he lives — the behavior of his gods, the facts of life and death, the ethics of his society, the way to success and happiness, the vagaries of human nature and the laws by which he must live — then proverbs must, indeed, fit the definition.

But, it may be contended, philosophy must entail abstract thought; and the primitive mind, so given to the use of proverbs, is incapable of such thinking. This kind of argument, however, does not carry very far, and is furthermore based upon a now outdated view of primitive mentality.[33] The argument itself is inappropriate since the proverbs must be judged apart from such preconceptions. If they clearly are expressions of abstract thought, then they give the lie to any view of primitive thinking which leaves no room for them. And any consideration of proverbial material, even that of primitive peoples, displays what cannot but be seen as abstract thinking. That is, primitive men have arrived at 'rules' or 'laws' of human behavior. They have abstracted from innumerable events certain generalizations. How else can one understand such examples as these from the Akan?

> You may have absolute liberty at your mother's hearth, but not at another's.[34]

> Anger is like a stranger, it does not stay in one house.[35]

> The slave naturally is always guilty.[36]

---

[33] Few today would insist that primitive modes of thought are essentially different from our own, and there is therefore no need to argue the point here. The *locus classicus* for the concept of a peculiar 'primitive mentality' is, of course, Lucien Levy-Bruhl's *Les Fonctions mentales dans les societes inferieures*, published in 1910. Paul Radin, among others, argued tellingly against this notion (see his *Primitive Man as Philosopher* cited above). And Levy-Bruhl himself seems to have abandoned the view before his death.

[34] Danquah, *op. cit.*, p. 188.

[35] *Op. cit.*,, p. 190.

[36] *Op. cit.*, p. 191.

If the elders are seeking to make it hot for you keep away from their fireplace.[37]

Or can one deny philosophical import to the following Bantu examples?

The earth is a beehive; we all enter by the same door but live in different cells. [38]

Where there is more than enough, more than enough is wasted.[39]

The journey of folly has to be travelled a second time.[40]

To-day's satiety is to-morrow's hunger.[41]

Sticks in a bundle are unbreakable.[42]

He who leaves a child lives eternally.[43]

These are not the conclusions of a sophisticated social philosophy, of course; but they do constitute, we submit, philosophical statements. They contain certain theorems which appear to operate within the world of social reality, and thereby serve to make it more comprehensible.

As Oesterley and Robinson have written in their *Hebrew Religion*,

The aim of all science and philosophy is the unification of experience, the reduction of all phenomena to a single rule, the discovery of a single fact or principle with which all the varied manifestations of the universe can be brought into accord. Its earliest effort at expression is normally in the epigram or proverb, a short saying in which a number of different facts are brought together, a generalization which shall include the results of a number of different observations. The wise man is he who has so observed life and the inter-relations of man and

37 *Op. cit.*, p. 195.
38 Champion, *op. cit.*, p. 509.
39 *Op. cit.*, p. 510.
40 *Op. cit.*, p. 511.
41 *Ibid.*
42 *Ibíd.*
43 *Op. cit.*, p. 512.

man, of man and nature, or of man and God, that he is able to group them, or many of them, under a single general 'law'. Such a law may be either descriptive of experience in the material world, when it will be an elementary form of natural science, or it may be normative of conduct when it will be a moral precept, or it may go deeper into the nature of reality when it will be classed as metaphysical.[44]

While one should not claim that the proverb attempts to unify *all* experience, the generalizing or abstracting function is clear.

T.H. Robinson has elsewhere discussed the proverb as a philosophical expression, and put the matter thus:

Such proverbs . . . may be described as the first tentative efforts of the human mind in the direction of a philosophy, and they are to be found almost everywhere. Regarded as the essence of human wisdom by generation after generation, they were quoted in market and field, in the city and in the open pasture. Learned men delighted in making collections of them, and it is interesting to note how often we find similar proverbs among peoples so far distant from one another as to preclude the idea of direct borrowing.[45]

In speaking of the proverb as a bearer of philosophical thought, one must remember that even as other creative insights are not merely the product of dispassionate speculation, so neither are those of the proverb-maker in all probability. One must allow, it would seem, for the creative moment of insight, for the dawning of awareness which comes unbidden to the thinking mind. Speculation there surely is, and careful observation; but it may be suggested that the moment at which a collection of impressions finally 'gels' into the proverb is frequently more than the end process of a particular line of thought.

The form of the proverb, we believe, is an indication of this creative, intuitive element. Just as we may observe the same stylistic features in both poetry and proverbs, and just as we can point to the same sort of psychological response on the part of the hearer, so may we quite naturally expect a corresponding similarity in the birth of the poem and the proverb. Just as the poet Houseman has said that "a

---

[44] W.O.E. Oesterley and Theodore H. Robinson, *Hebrew Religion* (New York: The Macmillan Company, 1930), p. 334.

[45] Theodore H. Robinson, *The Poetry of the Old Testament* (London: Duckworth, 1947), p. 165.

production of poetry is less an active than a passive and involuntary process", [46] so might we expect the genesis of the proverb frequently to be "passive and involuntary".

To put it another way, the proverb, while functioning as the bearer of philosophical insight, is often created in much the same way as the poem. And the hearer must bring his own experience to bear rather than follow out a logical argument. Professor Genung put the matter as follows more than a half-century ago:

In a sense this manner of statement may be regarded not as a contrast to, but a vigorous condensation of, the typical line of reasoning; something like the enthymeme as distinguished from the full syllogism. The conclusion is affirmed with uttermost emphasis; the process by which it is arrived at is left out. Between the analogy or sign which furnished the occasion and the full-orbed truth affirmed there is a gap for the reader or hearer to fill in; and so the latter is compelled to furnish the contribution of his own thought to the solution. [47]

Sub-Functions

Proverbs, in addition to possessing a general philosophical function, may be classified according to three main sub-functions: entertainment, instruction and legal usage. Each of these will be discussed separately:

Entertainment

Quite apart from the proverb's philosophical value it also frequently provides amusement to the hearer. The American dialect proverb, " 'Mean to' don't pick no cotton", possesses an amusing character in addition to its homiletical value. "The Chimpanzee could strut quite like a dandy but for his red buttocks" [48] is probably as amusing as instructive to the Akan listener. The Frenchman is probably amused

---

46 Ernst Kris, *Psychoanalytic Explorations in Art* (New York: International Universities Press, Inc., 1952), p. 295.
47 J.F. Genung, "The Development of Hebrew Wisdom", *The Biblical World*, Vol. XLII (July-December, 1913), p. 19.
48 Danquah, *op. cit.*, p. 192.

by "Donner une chandelle à Dieu et une (autre) au diable".[49] And the German smiles at his

Wer dem Kind die Nase wischt, küsst der Mutter den Backen.[50]

Sometimes we may expect that the learning of proverbs is carried on in the spirit of a game. The close relation between the riddle and the proverb has frequently been observed, and it is reported that in China the teacher of such wisdom would frequently recite the first line of the typical Chinese couplet proverb and allow the student to supply the second.[51] Apparently here we have a venerable tradition of 'making learning fun'. A similar use of proverbs has been noted by Loeb among the Kuanyama. He says that "a proverb is presented to a child or grown-up person, and he is expected to answer with another appropriate proverb".[52] The following example shows the kind of 'proverb-pair' which typically results:

Where fly birds is water;
Where laughs woman's laugh is kraal.[53]

Or, as Loeb puts it more freely,

Where one sees birds in their flight, there is water;
Where one hears the sound of women laughing, there is a kraal.[54]

Instruction

This leads to the consideration of a second sub-function of proverbs, the instruction of youth. Modern western society, of course, no longer makes extensive use of the proverb in this way. Yet probably such

49   de Guinzbourg, op cit., p. 53.
50   Kremer, op. cit., p. 61.
51   James A. Kelso, "Proverbs", Encyclopaedia of Religion and Ethics, ed. James Hastings, Vol. X, pp. 413, 415.
52   Loeb, op. cit., p. 332.
53   Ibid.
54   Ibid.

aphorisms as "Cleanliness is next to godliness" would not have been unusual in grandfather's grammar school.

But yet among less highly developed civilizations the proverb has continual use as an instrument of education. Loeb reports that "among the pagan Kuanyama, and in part among the Christians, much of the instruction given the young is in the form of proverbs, since these are easily remembered. The proverbs cover the realms of law, ethics, philosophy and religion".[55] That the proverb was used in Chinese instruction we have already noted. And indeed the content of most primitive proverbs makes clear their educational function: social ethics, personal responsibility, the facts of human nature – all are extensively reflected in primitive proverb lore.

Paul Clasper, former Vice-President of the Divinity School at Insein, Burma, reports from his experience that among the Burmese jungle people a large part of the culture is transmitted and preserved in the form of proverbs. In preaching to these people, he says, one of the most effective ways of establishing rapport is by reference to these popular maxims.[56]

Legal Usage

The third sub-function of the proverb is its use as a legal formulation. We hear not infrequently of law cases in Africa being decided by the aid of the proverb.[57] For example, these Kuanyama Ambo proverbs are so used: "A young chicken should scratch for its mother, your mother previously scratched for you".[58] Here is put forth the responsibility for the support of an aged mother. Or when one refuses to testify against a relative in court, this proverb can be cited: "Never shoot a bird which is resting on your own head (Never harm a relative or a member of the same clan)".[59]

In writing of the Jabo of Liberia, Herzog says, "The Africans are very legalistically minded. Since almost any act has legalistic aspects, there is hardly a discussion of any consequence (whether or not

---

55   Loeb, *op. cit.*, p. 322; See also Doke, *op. cit.*, p . XI.
56   Interview, March 2, 1964.
57   Franz Boas, *op. cit.*, p. 598; Doke, *op. cit.*, p. XI.
58   Loeb, *op. cit.*, p. 323.
59   *Op. cit.*, p . 322.

actually in court) in which proverbs are not employed."[60]

In discussing the legal use of proverbs in Indonesia, Loeb writes,

In Indonesia the *adat recht* (customary rights) is merely a collection of customs. The Indonesians themselves had no word for custom, but used the Arabic word *adat*. The real law of western Indonesia existed in former times, and still does to a considerable extent, in the form of proverbs. The patrilineal Bataks of Sumatra defend the rights of women by stating that 'a woman is no karabau, that she can be bought'. The neighboring Minangkabau, who are matrilineal, defend their system by stating that 'a rooster can lay no eggs'. Hence the father has no rights over his children, who belong to the mother's brother.[61]

We also hear of the use of proverbs in European law. For example, we read in a 14th century German legal tract, "Wherever you can attach a proverb, do so, for the peasants like to judge according to proverbs."[62] And in our own time we know a number of these legal proverbs: "Let the buyer beware" (German: "Augen auf, Kauf ist Kauf");[63] "Possession is nine points of the law"; "Ignorance of the law is no excuse"; [64] "Silence gives consent" ("Qui tacet, consentire vedetur");[65] "Two words to a bargain";[66] "Those who will not work shall not eat";[67] "My house is my castle";[68] "One witness is no witness" ("Ein Mann kein Mann", "Testis unus, testis nullus");[69] "A man who keeps a wife is like a man who keeps a monkey; he is responsible for her mischief".[70]

Such proverbs, of course, are not 'legislated', but appeal to them may be similar to appeal to 'cases'. For here one appeals to a kind of 'natural law', or 'what everyone knows'. In short the proverb carries a certain respected authority very much like that of a previous court decision.

60 Edwin Loeb, "The Function of Proverbs in the Intellectual Development of Primitive Peoples", *The Scientific Monthly*, Vol. LXXIV (February, 1952), p. 102.
61 *Ibid.*
62 Taylor, *op. cit.*, p . 87.
63 *Op. cit.*, p. 92.
64 *Op. cit.*, p. 93.
65 *Op. cit.*, p. 92.
66 *Op. cit.*, p. 90.
67 *Ibid.*
68 *Ibid.*
69 *Ibid.*
70 Champion, *op. cit.*, p. 44.

2. PROVERBS IN THE ANCIENT NEAR EAST

It is, of course, generally recognized that ancient Near Eastern Wisdom was a universal phenomenon. And the proverb, as an essential part of that wisdom, would also have been international in character.

Wisdom's international nature is no secret to the biblical writers, and there are several oft-cited passages which point to this fact. I Kings 4:30-31 tells us that "Solomon's wisdom surpassed all the wisdom of the people of the east, and all the wisdom of Egypt. For he was wiser than all other men, wiser than Ethan the Ezrahite, and Heman, Chalcol, and Darda, the sons of Mahol;[1] and his fame was in all the nations round about." We read of the wisdom of Edom,[2] the Phoenicians,[3] the Egyptians,[4] the Babylonians,[5] the Assyrians,[6] and even of the gentiles as a whole.[7] Job and his friends are in all probability not Israelites. And it is possible that Massa, mentioned in Prov. 30:1, was an Arab.[8]

To what extent we may speak of Arabic or Edomitic wisdom, however, is highly debatable. Pfeiffer would identify the whole skep-

---

1   Charles Fritsch identifies these men as "the Bedouin Arabs of the East, the land of Egypt, and the sons of Mahol, who were Edomite sages". Fritsch, "The Book of Proverbs . . .", p. 767. Albright, on the other hand, holds out for a Canaanite identification. William Foxwell Albright, *Archeology and the Religion of Israel* (Baltimore: Johns Hopkins Press, 1942), pp. 127-28.

2   Jer. 49:7; Obad. 8.

3   Ezek. 28; Zech. 9:2.

4   Isa. 19:11-15.

5   Isa. 44:25; 47:10; Jer. 50:35; 51:57.

6   Isa. 10:13.

7   Jer. 10:7.

8   Fritsch, "The Book of Proverbs . . .", p. 767.

tical side of Hebrew Wisdom as Edomitic in origin,[9] but would probably not convince many by his arguments. Furthermore, we lack the
kind of extra-biblical examples for the Arabs and Edomites that we
have for other cultures. In this paper, therefore, we shall content
ourselves with the mere mention of the biblical indications of this
desert-born wisdom, doubtful as some of them may be. Our principal
attention will be given to the evidence from ancient Egyptian, Babylonian, and Canaanite cultures.

Archeological discoveries over the past century have demonstrated
conclusively the existence of ancient Near Eastern wise men who were
influential in their respective cultures as far back as the third millennium B.C. That is, we know of scribes, the custodians of wisdom,
during this early period; and in fact we have two magnificent sculp-
tures of scribes dating from about 2500 B.C.: the Sumerian Dudu[10]
and his Egyptian counterpart.[11] As we shall see, these ancient writers
were acquainted with proverbial material; and if the proverb is originally an oral form rather than a literary one, as seems clear from its
simple, casy-to-remember structure and from what ethnologists have
noted in their studies of preliterate societies, then in all probability
this type of wisdom antedates even the invention of writing (fourth
millennium B.C. for early cuneiform).[12]

It seems clear that one can make no sharp distinction between the
scribe and the wise man of ancient times. The intelligentsia of Near
Eastern culture was composed of those who had been educated in the
scribal schools and who were then employed by the government in
clerical and administrative positions. They were, as has been frequently pointed out, in a class set apart.[13] We are fortunate in having, as a
result of archeological research, valuable evidence concerning the ancient scribe-wise-men of Egypt, Babylonia and Canaan. We shall look

9   Robert Pfeiffer, *Introduction to the Old Testament* (New York: Harper &
Brothers, 1948), p. 40.
10   James B. Pritchard, *The Ancient Near East in Pictures* (Princeton:
Princeton University Press, 1954), p. 40.
11   *Op. cit.*, p. 72.
12   Godfrey Rolles Driver, *Semitic Writing from Pictograph to Alphabet* (rev.
ed.; London: Oxford University Press, 1954), p. 7.
13   Adolph Erman, *The Literature of the Ancient Egyptians: Poems,
Narratives, and Manuals of Instruction from the Third and Second Millennia
B.C.*, trans. Aylward M. Blackman (London: Methuen & Co., 1927), p. xxvii.

at each of these old cultures separately, giving particular notice in each case to what the sages have left us with regard to their respective proverb traditions.

EGYPT

After the invention of writing in Egypt the development of the scribal class was to follow quickly. It will have been the mark of superior status to be able to read and write. And because of the administrative demands of a developing state this ability was the key to what we in our day should term 'upward mobility'. [14] The prominent officials of the Old Kingdom delighted to have themselves pictured in writing posture, "for that was the occupation to which they owed their rank and their power. The road to every office lay open to him who had learnt writing and knew how to express himself in well chosen terms, and all other professions were literally under his control." [15] The *Satire on Trades*, probably composed during the Middle Kingdom or earlier, makes abundantly clear the overweening scribal snobbery which then prevailed. In this composition, which was to become a standard copy-book example for budding scribes, the author spares no pains to tell us that only the scribe gets good, clean work. All other jobs, we are told, are miserable or degrading. The gossipy barber, the building contractor, the farmer, the fisherman, the odoriferous embalmer — all are pilloried.[16] And so the scribal student, as he learned to write, was also taught to appreciate the superiority of the vocation to which he aspired. "You see the worthy father leading his promising son to the boarding school where, in company with other young shoots of bureaucracy, he was to learn how to become a snob like his father and his companions." [17]

Furthermore, the scribal office was dignified with religious tradition, the god Thoth being revered as the inventer of writing, the

---

14   James Baikie, *A History of Egypt*, Vol. I (New York: The Macmillan Co., 1929), pp. 199-200.
15   Erman, *op. cit.*, pp. xxvii-xxviii. See also Hilaire Duesberg, *Les Scribes inspirés*, Vol. I (Paris: Desclée de Brouwer, 1938), p. 37.
16   James B. Pritchard, ed., *Ancient Near Eastern Texts*, 2nd ed. (Princeton: Princeton University Press, 1955), pp. 432-35.
17   Baikie, *op. cit.*, p. 357.

patron deity of the scribes and the principal inhabitant of the library.[18] "À Philé et à Dendérah sous les traits du singe, son image préside dans la salle des archives, et les scribes, qui la vénèrent, la placent dans les bureaux ministeriels."[19] In later centuries, however, much of the scribe's devotion was transferred to Imhotep, scribe and builder for the pharaoh Zeser, now become one of many famous scribes in Egyptian history.[20] As Baikie has described Imhotep,

Zeser's great servant had an even more distinguished destiny than his renowned master. The Pharaoh was worshipped; but in the end his councillor was actually deified. Age by age the reputation of the great architect and statesman grew. By the time of the rise of the Middle Kingdom his words were being quoted in songs as the ultimate expression of human wisdom; he became the typical wise man, philosopher, scribe, coiner of wise sayings, and physician; the scribe caste of Egypt looked to him as its patron saint; and the scribe poured out a libation to Imhotep before beginning any piece of writing. A temple was reared to his honor . . . . Finally the process of making a man into a god was accomplished by the acceptance of the Memphite belief that he was indeed the Son of God, being the offspring of Ptah, the Creator-God of Memphis, by a mortal mother.[21]

We may assume that Egyptian schools for scribes existed from the very earliest times. The needs of the state would have demanded them, and the large numbers of recovered ostraca bearing school-boys' exercises give ineloquent testimony to their existence.[22] One such school, attached to the Ramesseum at Thebes, has yielded up many of these ostraca bearing extracts from such ancient Egyptian classics as the *Instruction of King Amenemhet*, the *Instruction of Duauf* (*Satire on Trades*) and the *Hymn to the Nile*. We also have these books in complete form on two papyri of the same period, probably written in Memphis; and the papyrus copies are also school-boy exercises, even bearing marginal corrections made by the teachers.[23] While these

---

18   Duesberg, *op. cit.*, p. 42.
19   *Ibid.*; See also Alfred Bertholet, *A History of Hebrew Civilization*, trans. A.K. Dallas (London: George G. Harrop & Co. Ltd., 1926), p. 94.
20   Baikie, *op. cit.*, p. 96; Berthelot, *op. cit.*, p. 94.
21   Baikie, *op. cit.*, p. 97.
22   Duesberg, *op. cit.*, p. 53.
23   Millar Burrows, *What Mean These Stones?* (New Haven: American Schools of Oriental Research, 1941), p. 183.

copies are relatively late, the original works may date from the time of the Middle Kingdom or earlier.[24] From what we known of proverbial material, especially as an expression of pre-scientific philosophy, we may expect to find it carefully preserved and transmitted by the Egyptian scribes. It has not, however, come down to us in the kind of collections which are made in our time or which have been unearthed in the Sumerian excavations. Rather, what proverbs we have appear embedded within the instructive treatises attributed to old pharaohs and revered scribes.

These works, most of them well-known for several decades now, treat of the proper behavior for members of the scribal profession, and touch upon religion, ethics, diplomacy and even table manners. They are, in fact, manuals of what every young scribe should know if he is to be successful in life. These works have been extensively published and commented upon, and no purpose would be served in a detailed resumé here. It is our intent, however, to examine them for what light may be shed upon the form and function of the proverb in ancient Egypt.

Form

It has been shown that many of man's proverbs have what can be termed a poetic form, and appeal to us largely through that form. The proverbs of Egypt are no exception, and much of their poetic structure is still evident in English translation. Such devices as assonance and alliteration have been noted in the original language;[25] but they, of course, elude the English reader. Simile and metaphor are sometimes seen, but do not appear to be frequent.[26]

In addition to these almost incidental occurrences of simile and metaphor, however, we find extensive use made of parallelism, familiar to students of the Old Testament as a dominant feature of Hebrew poetry.[27] Examples of synonymous, antithetic and synthetic paral-

---

24   Pritchard, *Texts*, pp. 372, 432; Erman, *op. cit.*, pp. xxiv-xxv.

25   Erman, *op. cit.*, p. xxxiv.

26   Paul Humbert, *Recherches sur les Sources égyptiennes de la Littérature sapientiale d'Israël* (Neuchatel: Secrétariat de l'Université, 1929), p. 57.

27   See, for example, Norman K. Gottwald, "Poetry, Hebrew", *The Interpreter's Dictionary of the Bible*, eds. George Arthur Buttrick *et al.*, Vol. III

lelism can easily be located in such works as the *Instruction of the Vizier Ptahhotep*, the *Instruction of Amenomopet* and the *Instruction of Ani*.

It can be safely said, on the basis of the use of poetic forms, that these proverbs from ancient Egypt must be understood 'esthetically'. They, like so many of our own proverbs, make their point not by appeal to reason alone, but through their striking form. We also have good reason to believe on other grounds that form of expression came to be appreciated very early by the Egyptians. In one version of the *Instruction of Ptahhotep* we read this description of the contents: "The *beautifully expressed utterances* spoken by the vizier while instructing the ignorant *in knowledge and in the principles of elegant discourse*". [28] King Sneferu, in the Neferrohu papyrus, requests of his courtiers "*one that will speak to me beautiful words, choice speeches, in hearing which my majesty may find diversion*". [29]

In addition to these more poetic devices we meet certain other features in Egyptian Wisdom notable because of the Old Testament parallels: introduction of a proverb by the word "if", [30] value comparisons between two things ('better is . . . than . . .'), [31] etc. [32] But among these are two which are of particular interest: a negative construction characterized by the use of the imperative form or the simple negative, [33] and the positive imperative form. [34] We shall not discuss these usages here, but will have occasion to refer to them later.

Function

Even a cursory examination of the Egyptian documents reveals that same sort of philosophic function which has been seen to be the

---

(1962), pp. 829-38; George Buchanan Gray, *The Forms of Hebrew Poetry* (London: Hodder & Stoughton, 1915); Theodore H. Robinson, *op. cit.*

28   T.E. Peet, *A Comparative Study of the Literatures of Egypt, Palestine and Mesopotamia* (London: Oxford University Press, 1929), p. 129.

29   *Ibid.*

30   Humbert, *op. cit.*, p. 65.

31   *Op. cit.*, p. 66.

32   *Op. cit.*, pp. 52-74. A detailed discussion of a number of Egyptian parallels to biblical forms is presented here.

33   *Op. cit.*, p. 64.

34   *Op. cit.*, p. 66.

proper concern of proverbs everywhere. The one who quotes the proverb believes himself to be reflecting upon the established order of
human affairs. For those who hear and obey all will go well; disaster
lies in wait for those who turn aside.

Justice is great, and its appropriateness is lasting; it has not been
disturbed since the time of him who made it, (whereas) there is
punishment for him who passes over its laws . . . . Wrongdoing has
never brought its understanding into port.[35]

As for what we have referred to in Chapter 1 as sub-functions, the
Egyptian proverbial material presents an interesting picture. Everything appears to serve the purpose of instruction. By means of the
proverb form the young scribes are taught the values of successful
living and the morals of sound administration. And by comparison
with other proverb collections the Egyptian examples appear to be
almost entirely without humor.

Legal proverbs are present, but they would seem to lend themselves
more to teaching courtroom morals than to citation in legal cases.

BABYLONIA

When we turn to Babylonia we find very little in Akkadian that can be
classified as proverbs. Although we do have some translations from the
Sumerian, there have come to light no exclusively Akkadian proverb
collections and scarcely any isolated examples. We can do no better
than to quote W.G. Lambert at this point:

There is every indication that proverbs circulated in the Akkadian
language, but it is a curious phenomenon that they do not seem to
have become a part of stock literature. The only surviving tablets
written with collections of Babylonian proverbs are an Old Babylonian fragment, and two pieces found in the old Hittite capital at
Boghazköy, one of which was part of a Hittite rendering. The late
libraries, from which our knowledge of traditional Babylonian literature usually comes, have so far yielded not a single piece of Babylonian proverbs. The nearest approach to such is a late Babylonian

---

35   *Instruction of Ptahhotep*, Pritchard, *Texts*, p. 412.

exercise tablet which has four Babylonian proverbs among a hotch-potch of extracts used for writing exercises. This lack in the late librar-ies can hardly be explained by the accidents of discovery. Any day an old piece may turn up, but it is most unlikely that the general position will be altered. Babylonian proverbs are not a genre in the traditional literature of the Babylonians and Assyrians. The reason can be sug-gested. The codifiers of traditional literature during the Cassite period were very academic scholars, who may well have frowned on proverbs which were passed around among the uneducated. These scholars al-ready had a vast traditional genre of proverbs, Sumerian with Babylo-nian translations, which formed the proper study of the educated. Some of the bilingual proverbs in the Babylonian translation do in fact turn up in Akkadian texts . . ., so that the line between the two kinds is not rigorous.

The existence of a body of oral proverbs in Babylonian is shown by their occurrence in letters, works of literature, and elsewhere. Some are expressly given as proverbs (têltu), while others can be safely identified from a knowledge of them in other contexts.[36]

We should mention here a type of literature which, while not pro-verbial in any strict sense, closely resembles the didactic literature from Egypt. There is not an abundance of this material, and much of what is available is fragmentary in nature. The most important work of this kind for our consideration is the so-called *Counsels of Wisdom*. It is made up of ten separate sections, each devoted to a particular subject. Eight of the sections contain lines of four principal stresses; two contain lines of three. The work is addressed to "my son" after the fashion of so much Near Eastern wisdom, and it seems to refer to the proper behavior for one aspiring to a high administrative position. The work bears a close resemblance to that of Egypt and to some of our biblical proverbs. It comes, perhaps, from the second half of the second millennium B.C.[37]

As with Egyptian instruction, there is proverb-like material em-bedded within the text, and perhaps some of the sayings existed pre-viously in oral form. "The short sections and the epigrammatic nature of many of the lines would have made this text suitable for oral repetition, but we do not know definitely if, in part or whole, it enjoyed wide popular repute."[38]

---

[36]   W.G. Lambert, *Babylonian Wisdom Literature* (Oxford: The Clarendon Press, 1960), pp. 275-76.

[37]   *Op. cit.*, pp. 96-97.

[38]   *Op. cit.*, p. 97.

Our primary purpose for citing it here is to show the presence of negative and positive forms in the second person, not unlike those seen in Egyptian works:

> Do not utter libel, speak what is of good report.
> Do not say evil things, speak well of people.
> One who utters libel and speaks evil,
> Men will waylay him with his debit account to Šamaš.[39]

> Every day worship your god.
> Sacrifice and benediction are the proper accompaniment of incense.
> Present your free-will offering to your God,
> For this is proper toward the gods.[40]

> With a friend and comrade do not speak . .[. . .]
> Do not speak hypocrisy, [utter] what is decent.[41]

There are some interesting parallels between our biblical literature and the Aramaic *Words of Ahiqar*, probably of Assyrian origin. But the relative lateness of this work and the uncertainty of its provenance make it less suitable for our study than some other material. One interesting form needs to be cited, however, because of its similarity not only to Hebrew numerical proverbs, but to a similar Canaanite form. We shall have occasion to refer to this passage later:

> Two things [which] are meet, and the third pleasing to Shamash: One who dr[inks] wine and gives it to drink, one who guards wisdom, and one who hears a. word and does not tell.[42]

If the Babylonians thought little of the proverb, such does not seem to have been the case with their Sumerian predecessors. The Sumerians very definitely did make proverb collections, as we shall see; and "the Sumerian proverb collections antedate most, if not all, of the known Egyptian compilations by several centuries".[43]

39 *Op. cit.*, p. 105.
40 *Ibid.*
41 *Ibid.*
42 Pritchard, *Texts*, p. 428.
43 Kramer, *op. cit.*, p. 152.

Like their Egyptian counterparts the Sumerian proverbs appear to have come from the scribal schools, of which there were undoubtedly very many. Three possible school sites have been unearthed in Nippur, Sippar, and Ur; at any rate they were found to contain many tablets, which would not be expected in a normal home. A more school-like building emerged from the French Mari excavations of 1934-35, containing rows of baked brick benches; but unfortunately no tablets were to be found there! [44]

Furthermore, word-lists, seemingly compiled for teaching purposes, have come down to us from as far back as 3000 B.C. And from the middle of the third millenium B.C. we now possess a large number of school 'textbooks'. [45]

Just as in Egypt, ancient Sumer possessed an extensive scribal class devoted to the service of the temples and state administration and representing the wealthy ranks of society. [46] Here also the ability to read and write was the key to the lucrative positions of the state bureaucracy. As G.R. Driver has written, "The complex system of writing invented by the Sumerians and developed by the Akkadians was a 'secret treasure' or 'mystery' which the layman could not be expected to understand and which was therefore the peculiar possession of a professional class of clerks or scribes." [47]

Also like their Egyptian counterparts, the Sumerian scribes and their Akkadian successors were responsible for a kind of 'scribal cult'. They had their patron deity Nabû with his emblems of the tablet and wedge or, in some cases, the wedge alone. He it was who was credited with the invention of writing and referred to as the "unrivaled scribe" and "the scribe if the gods, wielder of the reed-pen". [48] One Nidaba or Nisaba was also revered as a heavenly scribe, as was her consort Hani or Haya; and both were sometimes referred to as patrons of learning. [49]

Some scribes, of course, became 'professors' and continued in the academic world throughout their lives. And it is probably to this intelligentsia that we owe much of the wealth of recorded myths,

44   *Op. cit.*, p. 8.
45   *Op. cit.*, p. 3. See also Duesberg, *op. cit.*, pp. 53-54.
46   Kramer, *op. cit.*, p. 5.
47   Driver, *op. cit.*, p. 62.
48   *Ibid.* See also Duesberg, *op. cit.*, p. 46.
49   Driver, *op. cit.*, p. 64.

epics, hymns, fables, essays and proverbs which are constantly coming to light.[50]

As for the proverbs themselves, literally hundreds have been recovered; but not all have been deciphered, published and translated. We have a small number of bi-lingual, Sumerian-Akkadian proverbs from the first millennium B.C. which have been known for some time.[51] In more recent years, however, through the efforts of Samuel Noah Kramer and Edmund Gordon, particularly the latter, our knowledge of the earlier Sumerian prototypes has been increased. Most of these latter proverbs have come to light since 1953. They come from the excavations at Nippur and date from the eighteenth century B.C.[52]

As a result of Gordon's recent work we now know of about seven hundred proverb-bearing tablets and fragments. Many of the tablets originally contained entire proverb collections. Others appear to be school practice tablets, and contain short extracts from collections or single proverbs.[53] It appears that the scribes of Sumer had compiled some fifteen to twenty standard proverb collections at least. And of these, ten or twelve can, for the most part, be reconstructed; and all in all we know of more than a thousand proverbs within these collections.[54]

It is too early to draw many definite conclusions about this ancient literature, since considerable work remains to be done and the translations are sometimes tentative. But by examining what is available,

---

50   Kramer, *op. cit.*, pp. 5-7.

51   Stephen Langdon published some of these in translation early in the century, but his work has now been superseded. See his "Babylonian Proverbs", *American Journal of Semitic Languages and Literatures*, Vol. XXVIII (July, 1912), pp. 217-43. Bruno Meissner also published some. See his *Die babylonisch-assyrische Literatur* (Wildpark-Potsdam: Akademische Verlagsgesellschaft Athenaion, 1927) or his *Babylonien und Assyrien II* (Heidelberg: Carl Winters Universitätsbuchhandlung, 1925).

52   Kramer, *op. cit.*, pp. 152-53; Samuel Noah Kramer, *The Sumerians, Their History, Culture, and Character* (Chicago: University of Chicago Press, 1963), p. 224.

53   Kramer, *The Sumerians...*, p. 224; Edmund I. Gordon, *Sumerian Proverbs: Glimpses of Everyday Life in Ancient Mesopotamia* (Philadelphia: The University Museum, 1959), p. 20.

54   Kramer, *The Sumerians...*, p. 224.

both in the Sumerian and the later bi-lingual sources, one may hazard some observations concerning the nature of Sumerian proverb lore.[55]

Form

When we look at the form of these Sumerian proverbs we find, as we might expect, that they exhibit figures of speech frequently associated with poetic usage. Gordon has located examples of metaphor, simile, hyperbole, metonymy and synecdoche.[56] Such devices as assonance, alliteration or rhyme cannot, of course, be seen in translation; and these forms seem not to have been commented upon.

We may cite the following examples of metaphor, including both internal metaphor and the external type, the latter depending upon its context for its point:

He who drinks much beer must drink water.[57]

He who eats too much cannot sleep.[58]

I am a lady of large garments; let me cut (?) my girdle.[59]

My eye is a lion, my figure is a protecting angel, my *hips* are absolute charm. Who will be my voluptuous spouse? [60]

Last year I ate garlic, this year my inside burns.[61]

[55]   Although the bi-lingual texts are several hundred years younger than the Sumerian, we may consider them together with a minimum of risk for the following reasons: (1) One may suppose that whatever the date of the tablet in question, a given proverb probably had a long previous oral history. (2) The fact that the bi-linguals are in part Sumerian points to their Sumerian origin. (3) For purposes of relating this material to biblical literature, one may assume a prior date in any event.

[56]   Gordon, *op. cit.*, pp. 14-15.

[57]   Edmund I Gordon, "The Sumerian Proverb Collection: A Preliminary Report", *Journal of the American Oriental Society*, Vol. LXXIV (April-June, 1954), p. 84.

[58]   *Ibid.*

[59]   *Op. cit.*, p. 85.

[60]   Lambert, *op. cit.*, p. 230.

[61]   *Op. cit.*, p. 249.

Possessions are sparrows in flight
which can find no place to alight.[62]

Kramer cites the following interesting specimens parallel to our "Don't count your chickens before they are hatched" and "Out of the frying pan, into the fire":

He did not catch the fox,
Yet he is making a neck-stock for it.[63]

Upon my escaping from the wild-ox,
The wild cow confronted me.[64]

The use of simile appears to be not nearly so extensive, but these examples can be found among the bi-linguals:

Like an old oven, it is hard to replace you.[65]

Like a fool [...] ..you perform your ablutions after sacrifice; like [......] .you put in a drain pipe after it has rained.[66]

The most important formal characteristic of the Sumerian proverb, however, is parallelism. Gordon writes of the two collections which he has edited, "Out of the nearly 300 proverbs here edited which are complete or sufficiently preserved for the recognition of their structure, 138 can be classified by the types of parallelism which they contain."[67]
The following are notable examples of antithetic parallelism:

Pleasure in drinking, fatigue on the road.[68]

---

62   Kramer, *The Sumerians . . .*, p. 225.
63   Kramer, *From the Tablets . . .*, p. 158.
64   *Ibid.*
65   Lambert, *op. cit.*, p. 250. See also J.J.A. van Dijk, *La Sagesse Suméro-Accadienne* (= *Commentationes Orientalis, Nederlandsch Instituut Voor Het Nabije Oosten*, Vol. I) (Leiden: E.J. Brill, 1953), p. 8.
66   Lambert, *op. cit.*, p. 282.
67   Gordon, *Sumerian Proverbs . . .*, p. 16.
68   Van Dijk, *loc. cit.*

Of what you have found you do not speak;
(Only) of what you have lost do you speak.[69]

What the weather might consume, the beasts have spared;
What the beasts might consume, the weather has spared.[70]

A chattering (?) maiden – her mother has silenced her;
A chattering (?) young man – his mother can (?) not silence him.[71]

The sick gets well; the healthy (?) becomes ill.[72]

When you have escaped, you are a wild bull.
When you have been caught, you fawn like a dog.[73]

The wise man is girded with a loincloth.
The fool is clad in a scarlet cloak.[74]

And here are a few passages illustrating parathetic or synonymous parallelism:

He who doesn't know drinking doesn't know what is good; drinking makes the house pleasant.[75]

It .is (only) a wild-ox in the nether world which does not eat food;
It is (only) a gazelle in the nether world which does not drink water.[76]

My mouth makes me comparable with men.
My mouth gets me reckoned among men.[77]

(The people of) a city – their hymns; a kid – its (being used for purposes of) extispicy.[78]

69 Gordon, *Sumerian Proverbs . . .*, p. 47.
70 *Op. cit.*, p. 51.
71 Gordon, "The Sumerian Proverb . . .", p. 85.
72 *Ibid.*
73 Lambert, *op. cit.*, p. 254.
74 *Op. cit.*, p. 232.
75 Van Dijk, *loc. cit.*
76 Gordon, *Sumerian Proverbs . . .*, p. 55.
77 Lambert, *op. cit.*, p. 238.
78 Gordon, *Sumerian Proverbs . . .*, p. 76.

Van Dijk notes this example, also cited above, as a synthetic-comparative type:

> Like an old oven, it is hard to replace you.[79]

A synonymously parallel comparative form is this one:

> A scribe without a hand (is like) a singer without a throat. (?)[80]

Of particular interest is a type of parallelism in which two parallel members precede a third 'climactic' element. Sometimes the first two elements may be in antithetic relation, but usually they are synonymous. And occasionally the 'climax' precedes two concluding parallel elements. Representing the antithetic type is this example:

> Tell a lie (and then) tell the truth: it will be considered (?) a lie.[81]

And the following proverbs illustrate the more common synonymous type:

> By marrying a thriftless wife, by begetting a thriftless son, un-unhappiness has become my store.[82]

> When a singer knows the hymns and performs well the trills (?), he is indeed a singer! [83]

> In a taunt is its taunt; in a curse is its curse. (Such is) the constant renewal of destiny! [84]

While there is some evidence of brief essays, this form does not seem to have been widely cultivated.[85]

---

79 Van Dijk, *loc. cit.*
80 Gordon, *Sumerian Proverbs . . .*, p. 204.
81 *Op. cit.*, p. 229.
82 *Op. cit.*, p. 119.
83 *Op. cit.*, 201.
84 *Op. cit.*, p. 82.
85 Kramer, *The Sumerians . . .*, p. 224; See also Samuel Noah Kramer,

There are among the Sumerian materials three collections of precepts and instructions;[86] they are of some importance, since they seem to be not unlike the well-known Egyptian instructions and parts of Proverbs. Of particular interest is the *Instruction of Shuruppak to His Son Zuisudra* "because of its stylistic device of ascribing whole wisdom collections to presumably very wise rulers of the distant past, a characteristic of the Biblical Book of Proverbs".[87] Furthermore, the introduction to this work reminds us very much of Egyptian and Hebrew wisdom:

> Shuruppak gave instructions to his son,
> Shuruppak, the son of Ubartutu,
> Gave instructions to his son Ziusudra:
>
> 'My son, I would instruct you, take my instruction,
> Ziusudra, I would utter a word to you, give heed to it;
> Do not neglect my instruction,
> Do not transgress the word I uttered,
> The father's instruction, the precious, carry out diligently'.[88]

From what we have seen there seems to be little doubt that these proverbs are very frequently poetic in nature and make their appeal largely through the use of poetic device. As Kramer has written, "Sumerian proverbs, like proverbs the world over, are brief pithy sayings which depend for their effect on extreme terseness of expression; on the unexpected turn of phrase; on evocation and connotation rather than straight statement of fact."[89]

Function

The function of the Sumerian aphorisms also indicates their kinship with the proverbs already discussed. They are generally philosophical in nature; they reflect the world as all men know it and as the ancient scribes observed it. Most of the examples cited in the above discussion

---

"Sumerian Wisdom Literature: A Preliminary Survey", *Bulletin of the American Schools of Oriental Research* No. 122 (April, 1951), p. 29.

86   Kramer, *The Sumerians . . .*, p. 224.
87   *Ibid.*
88   *Ibid.*
89   Kramer, "Sumerian Wisdom . . .", p. 29.

of form are illustrative of this function, but perhaps the following examples from the earliest proverbs make the point more effectively:

> The wealthy are distant (?), (but) poverty is at hand, is it not so (?)? [90]

> Merchandise which has become damaged (?) is no longer of interest (?) (lit., "has gone out from the heart").[91]

> The heart has not spawned hatred, (but) speech has spawned hatred.[92]

These two examples from the same time would seem to sound a more profound note:

> When fraud wears off, where will Utu (the sun-god) carry it (next)? [93]

> Whoever has walked with truth generates life.[94]

The following examples are from the bi-lingual collections:

> A people without a king (is like) a sheep without a shepherd.[95]

> Should I be going to die, I would be extravagant (lit. eat). Should I be going to survive, I would be economical (lit. store).[96]

> The will of a god cannot be understood, the way of a god cannot be known. Anything of a god is difficult to find out.[97]

These proverbs are, we submit, philosophical. As Samuel Noah Kramer has written in this regard,

90 Gordon, "The Sumerian Proverb . . .", p. 83.
91 *Ibid.*
92 *Op. cit.*, p. 84.
93 *Op. cit.*, p. 83; Gordon, *Sumerian Proverbs . . .,* p. 41.
94 Gordon, "The Sumerian Proverb . . .", p. 83; Gordon, *Sumerian Proverbs . . .,* p. 41.
95 Lambert, *op. cit.*, p. 232.
96 *Op. cit.* p. 250.
97 *Op. cit.*, p. 266.

The failure to distinguish between the Sumerian mythographer and philosopher has confused some of the modern students of ancient Oriental thought, particularly those strongly affected by the current demands for 'salvation' rather than 'truth', and has led them into both underestimating and overestimating the minds of the ancients. On the one hand, they argued, the ancients were incapable of thinking logically and intelligently on cosmic problems. On the other hand, they argued, the ancients were blessed with an intellectually 'unspoiled' mythopoetic mind, which was naturally profound and intuitive and could therefore penetrate cosmic truths far more perceptively than the modern mind with its analytic and intellectual approach. For the most part, this is just stuff and nonsense. The more mature and reflective Sumerian thinker had the mental capacity of thinking logically and coherently on any problems, including those concerned with the origin and operation of the universe.[98]

The most notable application of these proverbs was undoubtedly in instruction. From what we have seen of the prevalence of scribes and scribal schools this seems clear. Undoubtedly the proverbs were frequently used as exercises for copying, but we may assume that their lessons were to be taken seriously. Otherwise it would be difficult to explain the making of extensive collections. Surely these proverbs were not preserved merely as examples of spelling or 'stylusmanship'. The more specifically ethical injunctions would have been important in this regard, and one may well imagine the Sumerian schoolmaster imparting these bits of advice to his young scribelets:

> When you assert yourself, your god is yours. When you do not exert yourself, your god is not yours.[99]

> It is not wealth that is your support. It is (your) god.[100]

> The command of the palace is like Anu's: it may not be set aside. Like Šamaš', the king's word is sure, his command is unequalled, and his utterance cannot be altered.[101]

> Long life begets for you a sense of satisfaction; concealing a thing — sleepless worry; wealth — respect.[102]

98   Kramer, *From the Tablets . . .*, p. 76.
99   Lambert, *op. cit.*, p. 230.
100 *Op. cit.*, p. 232.
101 *Op. cit.*, p. 234.
102 *Op. cit.*, p. 253.

To converse with a blazing face, to become downcast, to concentrate one's attention on oneself — that is not human nature (as it should be).[103]

These examples, taken from the oldest tablets, are in the same vein:

Tell a lie; then if you tell the truth it will be deemed a lie.[104]

Build like a lord — live like a slave; build like a slave — live like a lord.[105]

A loving heart builds the home; a hating heart destroys the home.[106]

There appear to be no legal proverbs among the Sumerian collections studied. One, however, might be so used if Gordon's interpretation is correct:

It is a thing which is unprecedented (lit., "which did not exist in the past"); a young girl should not sit (?) in the lap of her spouse! (?) [107]

Gordon comments, "If the translation is correct, the fact that her husband is referred to may perhaps imply child-marriage, with a taboo against the usual marital relationships until a bride reaches puberty."[108] Another proverb, supporting this view, seems to criticize the practice of child-marriage:

I will not marry a wife who is only three years (old) as an ass (does)! [109]

If Gordon's is the proper interpretation, then the proverb might conceivably be cited in court.

103 *Op. cit.*, p. 269.
104 Kramer, *The Sumerians...*, p. 225.
105 *Ibid.*
106 *Op. cit.*, p. 226.
107 Gordon, "The Sumerian Proverb...", p. 83.
108 *Ibid.*
109 Gordon, *Sumerian Proverbs ...*, p. 235.

If humor was a characteristic of the Sumerian proverb, it has, for the most part, eluded us. The following example from the Nippur collection, cited above, might have amused the young scribes:

> I am a lady of large garments; let me cut (?) my girdle.[110]

And maybe to some these proto-Chaucerian gems were mirth-provoking:

> A thing which has not occurred since time immemorial: a young girl broke wind in her husband's bosom.[111]

> In respect to (both) expenditures and capital goods, the anus is great.[112]

> The anus breaks wind; the mouth chatters.[113]

In general, however, the laughter of the Sumerians must have been touched off by something other than their proverbs.

CANAAN

We have very little didactic literature from Canaan and almost no proverbs. But there is some scanty evidence of Canaanite proverbial material which is worth noting.

Irwin, while admitting the paucity of excavated wisdom literature, says that

the high attainments of their civilization, along with certain allusions and records in the Old Testament, make it quite clear that a vigorous, self-conscious wisdom movement had long functioned in Palestine before the Hebrews entered. And this fact is basic to an understanding of Israel's wisdom.[114]

---

110   Gordon, "The Sumerian Proverb . . .", p. 85.
111   Lambert, *op. cit.*, p. 260.
112   Edmund I. Gordon, "Sumerian Proverbs: Collection Four", *Journal of the American Oriental Society*, Vol. LXXVII (1957), p. 78.
113   *Ibid.*
114   William Irwin, "The Wisdom Literature", *Interpreter's Bible*, Vol. I, p. 213.

He goes on to indicate such evidence as the mention of a wise woman in Judg. 5:28-30 and II Sam. 14:1-20, the words of the wise woman in II Sam. 20:16-22 and her statement to the effect that the town Abel was renounded for wisdom. Samson's riddle and Jotham's fable, he says, also probably point to pre-Hebrew wisdom in Canaan.[115]

It was pointed out by Umberto Cassuto that forty word-pairs in parallelism existed in both Hebrew poetry and recently available texts from Ugarit. And Moshe Held has since collected some thirty additional examples.[116] In reporting upon the work of Cassuto and Held, Albright has written, "Even if we omit a few which are too general or not quite certain, we still have at least sixty such pairs of parallel words."[117] Parallels to some of these pairs have been located by Story in the book of Proverbs, as Albright points out;[118] but the examples are, unfortunately, not impressive. Such word-pairs as right and left, silver and gold, bread and wine, mouth and lips, hungry and thirsty, heaven and earth[119] might easily occur quite naturally in any literature which makes use of parallel forms. What is significant, however, is that parallelism as such was a familiar Canaanite device. Not only do we find words used in pairs, but also parallel meter: two beats to a unit, three beats to a unit, and some of the same metrical variations which are familiar in our canonical collection.[120]

Of particular interest are two Canaanite forms, pointed out by Story, which are similar to some biblical proverbs. The first is the use of a numerical form like those characteristic of Prov. 30:

Seven years may Baal fail, eight, the rider of clouds.[121]

We have already noted this same general form in our discussion of the

---

115 *Ibid.*
116 William Foxwell Albright, "Some Canaanite-Phoenician Sources of Hebrew Wisdom", *Wisdom in Israel and in the Ancient Near East*, eds. H.H. Rowley, Martin Noth, D. Winton Thomas (= Supplements to *Vetus Testamentum*, Vol. III) (Leiden: E.J. Brill, 1960), pp. 6-7.
117 *Op. cit.*, p. 7.
118 *Ibid.*
119 Cullen I.K. Story, "The Book of Proverbs and Northwest-Semitic Literature", *Journal of Biblical Literature*, Vol. LXIV (Sept., 1945), pp. 326-28.
120 *Op. cit.*, pp. 321-23.
121 *Op. cit.*, p. 324.

Words of Ahiqar.[122] Story also indicates a similarity in the use of a particular tricolon form such as is found in Prov. 10:26. Here is his Canaanite example:

> like the heart of the cow toward her calf,
> like the heart of the ewe toward her lamb,
> so is the heart of Anat toward Baal.[123]

We have already seen a form similar to this among the Sumerian examples.[124]

C.H. Gordon has written that "it should be stated that metric lengths, types of parallelism, strophic structures, etc., can be duplicated in the poetic books of the Old Testament."[125]

As for more direct evidence, Albright has identified two proverbs from the Amarna Letters as being basically Canaanite. The first is found in letter #252.

> If ants are smitten, they do not accept (the smiting) quietly, but they bite the hand of the man who smites them.[126]

The language of this passage, he says, is about twenty percent pure Akkadian, about forty percent mixed or ambiguous, and about forty percent pure Canaanite (disregarding the particle *u*, "and").[127] He similarly identifies this quotation of the Prince of Byblos, which occurs four times:

> My field (territory) is likened (mašil) to a woman without a husband, because it is not ploughed.[128]

While this evidence of Canaanite proverbs is not overwhelming, it does point to a Canaanite background for the poetic structure of Hebrew

---

122   Above, p. 43.
123   Story, *op. cit.*, p. 322.
124   Above, p. 49.
125   Quoted by Story, *op. cit.*, p. 321.
126   Albright, "Some Canaanite-Phoenician . . .", p. 7.
127   William Foxwell Albright, "An Archaic Hebrew Proverb in an Amarna Letter from Central Palestine", *Bulletin of the American Schools of Oriental Research*, Vol. LXXXIX (Feb., 1943), p. 29.
128   Albright, "Some Canaanite-Phoenician . . .", p. 7.

proverbs, or to a common Near Eastern poetic style. And the Amarna examples may indicate a considerable store of proverbs not now available to the scholar. Albright, in fact, has stated, "It can now be proved that substantial parts of proverbs are direct borrowings from Phoenician sources."[129]

EXTENDED USAGE

Up to this point we have, for the most part, been looking at proverbs as they occurred in collections and didactic treatises. If we look beyond this type of literature, however, we shall see that the proverb had an even wider influence. We have already seen that a couple of Canaanite proverbs are to be found among the Amarna Letters. But if we look a bit further afield in Egyptian and Babylonian literature, we find them cropping up there also.

The Egyptian *The Protests of the Eloquent Peasant* contains the following sayings, explicitly identified as proverbs:

> The name of the poor man is pronounced (only) for his master's sake.[130]

> Doing justice is the (very) breath of the nose.[131]

> Act for him who acts for thee.[132]

Within the same work there appear other examples which, while not conveniently labeled, may well be either proverb quotations or sentences patterned upon the proverb form:

> Punishment is short, (but) mischance is long.[133]

---

129   William Foxwell Albright, "The Role of the Canaanites in the History of Civilization", *The Bible and the Ancient Near East*, ed. G. Ernest Wright (Garden City: Doubleday & Co., Inc., 1961), p. 351.
130   Pritchard, *Texts*, p. 408.
131   *Op. cit.*, p. 409.
132   *Op. cit.*, p. 410.
133   *Op. cit.*, p. 409.

Do to the doer to cause him to do.[134]

That great one who is covetous is not really great.[135]

There is no yesterday for the slothful.[136]

In the Akkadian *"I Will Praise the Lord of Wisdom"* we have this probable proverb:

What is good in one man's sight is evil for a god.
What is bad in one's own mind is good for his god.[137]

The Akkadian *A Pessimistic Dialogue Between Master and Servant* displays what may be the use of contradictory proverbs by the vascillating servant. Each time the master expresses a desire, his servant expresses his approval. When the master then changes his mind, the servant cheerfully endorses the about-face. And in some of his responses he seems to employ proverbs.

134   *Ibid.*
135   *Ibid.*
136   *Ibid.*
137   *Op. cit.*, p. 435.

3. PROVERBS IN ISRAEL

Having looked at the proverb form in general, as we know it and as it exists in primitive cultures, and having examined the role of proverbs in non-Hebrew cultures of the ancient Near East, we now turn to a consideration of the proverbs of Israel. In both the Old Testament and the Apocrypha the pervasiveness of the proverb's influence is apparent. From as far back as the early monarchy come some popular examples, and others may be even earlier. The Hebrew sages of later times, like the wise men of neighboring cultures, used proverbs in their teaching, turned to them as embodiments of ancient and reliable wisdom, collected and edited them, and even added to them out of their own observations and creative efforts. The collections contained in our canonical Proverbs bear eloquent witness to their scholarly endeavors. But proverbs were also important in their more occasional usage in Psalms, in the word of the Prophets, in legal material, in the biblical wisdom books of Ecclesiastes and Job, and in the wisdom literature of the Apocrypha: Ecclesiasticus and the Wisdom of Solomon.

We shall have occasion to note the proverb's influence in each of these areas or books during the course of our discussion in Chapters 3, 4 and 5. But now we turn to a general treatment of the form and function of the Hebrew proverb in general.

FORM

It has frequently been noted that among Israel's proverbs a clear distinction can be made between the popular proverb and the more polished literary aphorism typical of the book of Proverbs.[1] And

---

1   Bertholet, *op. cit.*, pp. 329-30; Thomas Kelly Cheyne, *Job and Solomon; or*

indeed, if we examine the other literature of the Bible we find a number of examples of this popular type. In I Sam. 24:13 the words "Out of the wicked comes forth wickedness" are quoted as a "proverb of the ancients". "Let them ask counsel at Abel" is repeated in II Sam. 20:18 as an adage which "they were wont to say in old time". We have what appears to be an old popular proverb in I Kings 20:11: "Let not him that girds on his armor boast himself as he that puts it off." In Gen. 10:9, a relatively late (P) passage, we have what may be a very early proverbial saying: "Like Nimrod a mighty hunter before the LORD." And in Jer. 31:29 and Ezek. 18:2 there is quoted the popular maxim, "The fathers have eaten sour grapes and the children's teeth are set on edge."

Coming probably from the period of the early monarchy we have the proverbial saying, "Is Saul also among the prophets?"; and in I Sam. we have two different accounts of its origin.[2] In II Sam. 5:8 we have what appears to be the origin of another popular proverb from the same period: "And David said on that day, 'Whoever would smite the Jebusites, let him get up the water shaft to attack the lame and the blind, who are hated by David's soul.' Therefore it is said, 'The blind and the lame shall not come into the house.' "

How old these proverbs are, or who first uttered them, we shall never know. Perhaps those sayings purporting to stem from an historical event did in fact do so; but the conflicting accounts of I Sam. 10:12; 19:24 make even this possibility uncertain. In any event the popular adage appears to have been quite at home in ancient Israel. And since the inclusion of these proverbs is almost incidental in the historical narratives, we may suppose that there existed a sizable fund of oral material upon which to draw. Indeed, if we may speculate upon what we have seen of the popularity of the proverb in primitive cultures of our time, we should expect it to be so.

When we turn to the canonical book of Proverbs we encounter in abundance the parallel forms typical of Hebrew poetry. Examples of

---

the Wisdom of the Old Testament (London: Kegan Paul, Trench, & Co., 1887), pp. 125-26; Otto Eissfeldt, *Einleitung in das Alte Testament*, 3[e] neubearbeitete Auflage (*Neue Theologische Grundrisse*) (Tübingen: J.Ç.B. Mohr, 1964), pp. 109-15; Johannes Hempel, *Althebräische Literatur und ihre hellenistisch-jüdisches Nachleben* (Wildpark-Potsdam: Akademische Verlagsgesellschaft, 1930), pp. 44-50.
2   I Sam 10:12; 19:24.

antithetic parallelism are abundant, particularly as the wise man is contrasted with the fool, or the righteous with the wicked:

> A prudent man conceals his knowledge,
> but fools proclaim their folly.[3]

> The wicked are overthrown and are no more,
> but the house of the righteous will stand.[4]

Synonymous parallelism is also prevalent:

> An evildoer listens to wicked lips;
> and a liar gives heed to a mischievous tongue.[5]

Synthetic parallelism is not unusual:

> The LORD has made everything for its purpose,
> even the wicked for the day of trouble.[6]

And comparative parallelism is also seen:

> Like clouds and wind without rain is a man who boasts of a gift
> he does not give.[7]

In fact, as is almost always pointed out in studies of Proverbs, the single parallel couplet is basic to the structure of the entire book and fundamental to the second, or artistic type of the Hebrew proverb. Even the more expanded essay form, so characteristic of the earlier chapters, is made up of parallel couplet 'building blocks'. While the recognition of this basic form in proverbs is important to our study, and will be discussed later in relation to non-Hebrew usage, a detailed treatment here of what is so well-known would be tedious and unnecessary.[8]

---

3 Prov. 12:23.
4 Prov. 12:7.
5 Prov. 17:4.
6 Prov. 16:4.
7 Prov. 25:14.
8 For an exhaustive study of this form see Johannes Schmidt, *Studien zur Stilistik der alttestamentlichen Spruchliteratur* (= Alttestamentliche Abhandlungen, XIII. Band, 1. Heft) (Münster: Verlag der Aschendorffschen Verlagsbuchhandlung, 1936).

4 FORMS

However, in anticipation of later discussion, four particular forms should be pointed out. The first of these is a form of couplet in which two synonymously parallel parts of the first stich stand in comparative parallelism with the climactic second stich:

> Like vinegar to the teeth, and smoke to the eyes,
> so is the sluggard to those who send him.[9]

A second form is the comparative type of the "Better is A than B" variety, noted by Humbert in Egyptian Wisdom:[10]

> Better is a man of humble standing who works for himself
> than one who plays the great man but lacks bread.[11]

The third form is the numerical proverb, characteristic of Prov. 30, which begins by stating one number less than the total number to be considered:

> Under three things the earth trembles;
> under four it cannot bear up:
> a slave when he becomes king,
> and a fool when he is filled with food;
> an unloved woman when she gets a husband,
> and a maid when she succeeds her mistress.[12]

The fourth type is the second person form, sometimes negative and sometimes positive. We have mentioned this as also characteristic of the Egyptian material, but have deferred discussion for a later treatment. We have also seen that the form was known in Babylonian Wisdom. These examples from Proverbs are in the same general style:

> Leave the presence of a fool,
> for there you do not meet words of knowledge.[13]

---

9   Prov. 10:26; cf., Prov. 25:26, 26:2; 26:21.
10   Above, p. 40.
11   Prov. 12:9.
12   Prov. 30:21-23.
13   Prov. 14:7.

Do not rob the poor, because he is poor,
or crush the afflicted at the gate;[14]
. . . .

It is significant that our Proverbs has a concentration of these forms in 22:17-24:22, the material most closely related to the *Instruction of Amenemopet*. We shall see in Chapter 4 what appears to be a major influence of this form upon Israel's legal tradition.

In addition to such forms as these we find in Proverbs the extended use of metaphor and simile. "A good wife is the crown of her husband . . .",[15] "A gentle tongue is a tree of life . . .";[16] "Wine is a mocker, strong drink a brawler . . .";[17] A worthless man's "speech is like a scorching fire";[18] "The purpose in a man's mind is like deep water . . ."[19] In the examples of simile cited here the Hebrew has the particle כְּ. And yet this is not always expressed. It is not present, for example, in 17:8: "A bribe is like a magic stone in the eyes of him who gives it . . ." Apparently our distinction between metaphor and simile is not appropriate here. The use of some inclusive word like 'similitude'[20] is undoubtedly better.

Such other devices as alliteration, assonance and rhyme should also be noted as characteristic of Proverbs,[21] although one finds less frequent reference to such usage than one might expect. Just how extensively these devices are employed, however, would seem to be a matter for debate. Gemser, following Boström and others, says that in almost every verse of Proverbs some form of paronomasia is to be found.[22] Yet one wonders whether our present knowledge of the

---

14   Prov. 22:22.
15   Prov. 12:4.
16   Prov. 15:4.
17   Prov. 20:1.
18   Prov. 16:27.
19   Prov. 20:5.
20   See Charles Foster Kent, *The Wise Men of Ancient Israel and Their Proverbs* (Boston: Silver, Burdett & Co., 1895), p. 33.
21   Johannes Hempel, "The Forms of Oral Tradition", *Record and Revelation*, ed. H. Wheeler Robinson (Oxford: At the Clarendon Press, 1938), p. 35; Robinson, *op. cit.* p. 172; E.T. Ryder, "Form Criticism of the Old Testament", *Peake's Commentary on the Bible*, eds. Matthew Black and H.H. Rowley (London: Thomas Nelson and Sons, 1962), p. 94.
22   Gemser, *op cit.*, p. 5.

original vocalization of Hebrew allows for such an extreme asser-
tion.[23] Apart from the question of frequency, however, the presence
of such devices is not a matter for argument. The alliteration and
assonance of Prov. 15:27a, for example, are unmistakable:

עֹכֵר בֵּיתוֹ בּוֹצֵעַ בָּצַע

The assonance of Prov. 10:9a is almost as evident:

הוֹלֵךְ בַּתֹּם יֵלֶךְ בֶּטַח

Toy points out the assonance of Prov. 13:20b:[24]

וְרֹעֶה כְסִילִים יֵרוֹעַ

And Gemser notes, among other examples, the paronomasia in Prov.
22:24:[25]

אַל־תִּתְרַע אֶת־בַּעַל אָף

וְאֶת־אִישׁ חֵמוֹת לֹא תָבוֹא

Even end rhyme seems to have been a device of the proverb-makers:

[26]
בָּא זָדוֹן וַיָּבֹא קָלוֹן
נֹצֵר פִּיו שֹׁמֵר נַפְשׁוֹ

[27]
יֹשֵׁק שְׂפָתַיִם מֵשִׁיב נְכֹחִים

---

23 Bentzen, op. cit., Vol. I, p. 175.
24 Crawford H. Toy, A Critical and Exegetical Commentary on the Book of
Proverbs (The International Critical Commentary) (New York: Charles Scribner's Sons, 1916), p. 275.
25 Gemser, loc. cit.
26 Prov. 11:2a.
27 Prov. 13:3. For further examples of rhyme see Otto Eissfeldt, "Der
Maschal im Alten Testament", Beihefte zur Zeitschrift für die alttestamentliche
Wissenschaft, Vol. XXIV (Geissen: Alfred Töpelmann, 1913), p. 49.

It is important to recognize the presence of these less frequently mentioned characteristics of Proverbs for two reasons. In the first place one may thereby be helped in the matter of textual correction. Oesterley, for example, reconstructs the corrupt Hebrew of Prov. 15:9 in part on the basis of establishing a probable play on words.[28] Whether we accept his emendations, or not, the consideration of a likely wordplay is quite legitimate. One should also be wary of demanding too much logic and precision from a given passage. In commenting upon 10:13, for example, Toy notes: "The two clauses, taken separately, give each a good sense, but there is no close connection between them."[29] Consequently he regards the second clause as dislocated. We should affirm, however, that the connection is seen in the assonance of the initial words in each stich:

בְּשִׂפְתֵי נָבוֹן תִּמָּצֵא חָכְמָה

וְשֵׁבֶט לְגֵו חֲסַר־לֵב.

That each part may have once circulated separately we should not deny. But that these two become associated by the בְּשִׂפְתֵי־וְשֵׁבֶט assonance and so 'belong together' we think highly likely. The matter of such couplet formation is a problem unto itself and will be taken up later in our discussion of function.

But in addition to indicating such critical concerns, it must also be said that Proverbs loses a great deal in translation. We have noted in Chapter 1 the importance of sound and hearing for the proverb in general; these considerations are no less important for Hebrew aphorisms. The skillfully turned phrase of Prov. 15:27a, cited above, comes across in The Revised Standard Version as follows:

> He who is greedy for unjust gain makes trouble for his household.

For such stichs as this, we submit, form means almost everything!

---

28 W.O.E. Oesterley, *The Book of Proverbs* (New York: E.P. Dutton and Co., Inc., 1929), p. 108.
29 Toy, *op. cit.*, p. 207.

That the poetic form of these proverbs is of the greatest significance should be clear from our discussion of proverbs in general. And
in fact it has not gone unnoticed by scholars. Gemser has written with
regard to paronomasia in Proverbs,

Dabei ist die Paronomasie nicht nur ein Wort-und-Klangspiel, sondern
hat nach antiker Auffassung auch gedankenbildende, erklärende und
überzeugende Kraft . . . eine Tatsache, die den Zusammenhang von
מָשָׁל 'Spruch' und מָשַׁל 'Herrschen' verständlich macht. Der
Maschal ist ein krafterfülltes Wort, etwas was über das Gewöhnliche
hinausgeht . . .[30]

And Rylaarsdam says,

In many ways the sages make clear in Prov. that their words establish
a standard. The authority consists not only in the tested quality of the
pronouncements but is also displayed in and certified by the literary
style of their work. The terseness, the economy of words, assonance,
and the accent of rhythm all figure in this close bond between form
and reality as assumed in Prov.[31]

Having considered the popular proverb and the more polished variety
of the book of Proverbs, it remains to be considered whether the
distinction between the two types is an entirely satisfactory one. Although we are compelled to see in the thoroughgoing use of parallelism the influence of the wise man, it would seem best not to press
the distinction too far. Eissfeldt points out that some old popular
proverbs, difficult to distinguish from prose, have turned up within
the book of Proverbs, there provided with varying parallel stichs:
10:15 and 18:11; 11:13 and 20:19.[32] Schmidt would see the *Volks-
weisheitsprüche* as forming the nucleus of many of the verses of
Proverbs,[33] and von Rad would concur in this.[34] Bentzen states with

---

30 Gemser, *op cit.*, p. 7.
31 J. Coert Rylaarsdam, "The Proverbs", *Peake's Commentary on the Bible*,
eds. Matthew Black and H.H. Rowley (London: Thomas Nelson and Sons Ltd.,
1962), p. 444.
32 Eissfeldt, *Einleitung . . .* , p. 110.
33 Schmidt, *op. cit.*, p. 27.
34 Gerhard von Rad, *Old Testament Theology*, Vol. I, trans. D.M.G. Stalker
(Edinburgh: Oliver and Boyd, 1962), p. 430.

regard to the parallel proverb that, "it is generally assumed that it has some relation to the popular proverb".[35] Hylmö holds, in Bentzen's words, that "setting aside a few proverbs preserved in the books of the prophets — *the popular proverbs have no poetical form*, neither parallelism nor rhythm . . .".[36] But given a popular, one-line prose proverb, one can easily imagine its becoming poetic through the addition of a parallel stich;[37] and one may suspect that this often happened. There are, in addition to those just mentioned, several instances in which one stich appears with one or more different parallel companions.[38] But the determination of which stichs were popular in origin and which were not — this would be in our opinion quite impossible. As a matter of fact our biblical proverb collection is not the only one to present such an ambiguous picture. Writing of the two Sumerian proverb collections which he had studied intensively, Gordon says that

there are a number of indications pointing to the original composition of many of these proverbs by the Sumerian *literati* of the Edubba, the Sumerian academies, although there is some reason to believe that at least some of the proverbs were collected by the scribes from 'out of the mouth of the people'.[39]

We have seen, moreover, how a type of parallelism has developed out of popular practice.[40] And we cannot assume, it seems, that this did not sometimes take place among the ordinary folk of ancient Israel.

But in addition to the probability of the popular proverb's having been absorbed into the literature of the wise, one may also suspect that the process could take place in the other direction. Both Jeremiah and Ezekiel quote as a *popular* parallel proverb the saying, "The fathers have eaten sour grapes, and the children's teeth are set on edge."[41] This may have been a popular creation, of course; but it also may have derived from the circles of the wise. There is a democratic

---

35   Bentzen, *op. cit.,* Vol. I, p. 167.
36   *Op. cit.*, p. 168.
37   See Schmidt, *op. cit.*, pp. 12-17.
38   Gemser, *op. cit.*, p. 45.
39   Gordon, *Sumerian Proverbs*, p. 19.
40   Above, p. 32.
41   Jer. 31:29; Ezek. 18:2.

spirit in our book of Proverbs and an absence of the emphasis upon scribal privilege so evident in Egyptian and Babylonian wisdom. And there is certainly no evidence that Israel's wisdom was at all esoteric. It seems, then, quite possible that the stylized sayings of the wise may frequently have become common coin.

To conclude our discussion of form we may say that the extensive use of parallelism in our book of Proverbs would seem to indicate the activities of the Hebrew wise men. Beyond this, however, we must confess our inability to determine in most cases whether a given proverb is their creation or not.

FUNCTION

The basic function of Hebrew proverbs, as with all proverbs, appears to be philosophical. It must be remembered, however, that the use of the term does not imply the type of systematic thinking common to Western philosophical traditions. But, as Beecher wrote at the end of the last century about wisdom literature in general,

if a keen and genuine and fruitful study of the universe and the purposes for which we are in it constitutes a philosophy, irrespective of conventional lines and methods, then this literature is in the highest degree philosophical, and its *hākām*, its 'wise man' is above all others the man who has a Philosophy of life.[42]

von Rad has seen this function of the early popular proverb in Israel as dealing with "a practical knowledge of the laws of life and of the world, based upon experience".[43]

But unlike so much of what we should term 'philosophy', most of the Hebrew proverbs demonstrate a more profound connection between content and form. Their 'truth value' is intimately connected with their poetic structure. As von Rad has written, "The assonant form   באָ לָדוֹן וִיפֹא מַלוֹן   , Prov. XI 2) again reminds us what outstanding importance attaches to the word that pins down

---

42   W.J. Beecher, "The Wisdom Literature", *The Bible as Literature*, ed. Richard Green Moulton *et al.*, 6th ed. (New York: Thomas Y. Crowell & Co., 1896), p. 115.
43   von Rad, *op. cit.*, p. 418.

these general truths — only by being formulated is the truth given its sanction." [44] He goes on to quote from W. Preisendanz's *Die Spruch-form in der Lyrik des alten Goethe und ihre Vorgeschichte seit Opitz*: "With a proverb what alone gives the content significance is the form, be that never so primitive or bizarre . . . This means that with a pro-verb it is a matter of a truth which is only given its sanction by the form . . ."[45] Artur Weiser has said much the same thing with regard to Hebrew poetry in general, but unfortunately implies a restriction to the primitive thought world:

According to primitive ideas the fixed formula, determined according to the wording, the sound and the rhythm, had ascribed to it a special power and effective force which the simple word did not possess. The ability to grapple successfully with certain situations in life depended upon the knowledge of the right formula, the correct pronunciation of the *verba certa*, the 'set words': this is one of the main roots of all poetic tradition.[46]

We have noted in Chapter 1 that it is not only the primitive mind that is captivated by poetic proverb form, but we may probably assume that the primitive attached considerably greater significance to the poetic word than we do.

Furthermore, the truth so preserved is not simply the product of detached speculation but of careful observation and generalization. A regularity in the natural order or in human relations is learned by experience and then fixed in the form of a proverb. If it contradicts other truths, similarly fixed, then so be it. The old Hebrew was not compelled to reconcile the contradictions which he perceived, but in fact seems to have taken a delight in noting them. He could place side by side such disparate proverbs as these:

> Answer not a fool according to his folly,
>   lest you be like him yourself,
> Answer a fool according to his folly,
>   lest he be wise in his own eyes.[47]

---

44   *Op. cit.*, p. 419; See also Hempel, "The Forms . . .", p. 35.
45   von Rad, *op. cit.*, p. 419.
46   Artur Weiser, *The Old Testament: Its Formation and Development*, trans. Dorothea M. Barton (New York: Association Press, 1961), p. 23.
47   Prov. 26:4-5.

Each is true, but only under certain circumstances. Each has captured in the magic of its form a 'moment of truth', recognized by the hearer, capable of being applied by him, but not applicable in every confrontation with a fool. We are here reminded of similar contradictions among our own proverbs. For example, we may be told that "He who hesitates is lost", and "Look before you leap". In Japan one may affirm, on the one hand, that "A wife and a floor mat are good when fresh and new", or on the other hand that "A wife and kettle get better as they grow older". [48]

Thus we have in our Hebrew proverbs, as in others, isolated insights given permanence and power through unique forms. They are, however, limited and incomplete by comparison with any unified understanding of the world. As von Rad has put it so well:

Now, when we bear in mind that every people expended a great deal of trouble and artistry in the formation of this kind of Wisdom literature, and the gnomic apperception is in fact one of the most elegant forms of human thinking and a weapon in the struggle for spiritual content in life, it will be apparent that there are two completely different forms of the apperception of truth for mankind — one systematic (philosophical and theological) and one empirical and gnomic. Each requires the other. Where the one employed by the Wisdom literature is wanting, men are in danger of reducing everything to dogma, and indeed of running off into ideological fantasy. Empirical and gnomic wisdom starts from the unyielding presupposition that there is a hidden order in things and events — only, it has to be discerned in them, with great patience and at the cost of all kinds of painful experience. And this order is kindly and righteous. But, characteristically, it is not understood systematically — and therefore not in such a way as to reduce all the variety experienced and perceived to a general principle of order, and least of by the search for a formula which might be spacious enough to comprehend the infinitely varied world of phenomena. This would be the philosophic and systematic way. [49]

von Rad obviously here retains the narrower, Western concept of 'philosophy', but in his discussion of "empirical and gnomic" wisdom includes what we have talked about within the broader definition.

48   Mario Pei, "Parallel Proverbs", *Saturday Review* (May 2, 1964), p. 17.
49   von Rad, *op. cit.*, pp. 421-22.

Another feature of the Hebrew proverb, particularly notable in comparative parallelism, is a kind of reasoning by analogy. We have noted that the proverb presupposes a basic order in the universe; here it moves from one sphere of this order to another, most commonly from the order of nature to the order of human relationships. It is as though the proverb-maker were telling us that order in one realm has some mysterious correspondence to order in the other, or that a breach of proper order in one sphere corresponds to a similar breach in the other:[50]

> Like a sparrow in its flitting, like a swallow in its flying,
> a curse that is causeless does not alight.[51]

> Like a bird that strays from its nest
> is a man who strays from his home.[52]

> Like clouds and wind without rain
> is a man who boasts of a gift he does not give.[53]

One must not push this correspondence too far, however. Other analogies appear to be pure stylistic:

> As a door turns on its hinges,
> so does a sluggard on his bed.[54]

> The words of a whisperer are like delicious morsels;
> they go down into the inner parts of the body.[55]

We have noted that peculiar form which, in the Bible, occurs in Prov. 30, [56] but which, as we have seen, is not peculiar to Hebrew literature: the numerical proverb. It, too, according to von Rad, exemplifies a very ancient attempt by man to order his universe, to make categories,

---

50   *Op. cit.*, pp. 424-25.
51   Prov. 26:2.
52   Prov. 27:8.
53   Prov. 26:14.
54   Prov. 27:14.
55   Prov. 26:22.
56   Above, p. 62.

and thereby get a grasp on the reality underlying the phenomenal world. [57] Four things are alike in their mystery: ". . . the way of an eagle in the sky, the way of a serpent on the rock, the way of a ship on the high seas, and the way of a man with a maiden". [58] And four things are alike in being both small and wise: ants, badgers, locusts and lizards. [59] von Rad says that "these puzzling things must somehow be mastered conceptually, and this is achieved by ranging them in categories. When like can be set alongside like, there is already great gain, for these phenomena now lose the absolutely puzzling quality that they had in isolation."[60]

A further philosophical characteristic of Hebrew proverbs is their appeal to human reason and human experience. They are concerned primarily with human welfare and human understanding. They point to the natural capacities of man to comprehend and control his world. We find here no clear-cut categorical demands for obedience either to an immutable law or to the sovereign will of God. [61] As Zimmerli has demonstrated, obedience is not the virtue of wisdom, but תבונה and דעת, דעת signifying not the knowledge of God, as in Jeremiah and Hosea, but the faculty of weighing, skill in deliberation.[62] He points out that such contradictory statements as those in Prov. 26:4-5, cited above,[63] make no sense as categorical demands, but only as appeals to the ability of man to size up a situation and make proper application according to his own good sense.[64] Von Rad makes the same point when he writes,

---

57   von Rad, *op. cit.*, p. 425.
58   Prov. 30:18-19.
59   Prov. 30:24-28.
60   von Rad, *op. cit.*, p. 425. See also O.P. Dubarle, *Les Sages d'Israël* (Paris: Les Éditions Cerf, 1946), p. 59.
61   W. Zimmerli, "Zur Struktur der alttestamentlichen Weisheit", *Zeitschrift für die alttestamentliche Wissenschaft*, Vol. LI (1933), pp. 177-92. This is also true of the simple second person injunction, which might at first seem to be an exception. It is so general as to leave specific understanding and application to the hearer.
62   *Op. cit.*, p. 183.
63   Above, p. 69.
64   Zimmerli, *op. cit .*, p. 188.

Here the wisdom teacher wanted to help the young man to preserve his strength and fortune and to safeguard his manhood. But he did not do so with divine commandments: these he had no authority to give, for his counsels were of course derived essentially from experience. In consequence what he could help the young man with were only 'pieces of advice' (עצה). Such counsel does not demand obedience, but it asks to be tested: it appeals to the judgment of the hearer; it is intended to be understood, and to make decisions easier.[65]

It is true that some proverbs make reference to God and to his will: Prov. 17:5; 20:23; 11:20; but these references are not characteristic of the book as a whole, and they seem to indicate that God is a factor to be reckoned with rather than a sovereign to be obeyed. As Zimmerli has said, the creative power of God is often stressed and his supreme position is not questioned. But at the same time the fear of God and the blessing of God are intimately related to such human goods as wealth, life, security, honor. Man with his potentialities continues to occupy the center of the stage. There is, as it were, a calculable side to God's action; it is Wisdom's virtue to have some insight into how man can live in God's favor. But she has this knowledge as a result of human reflection and experience, not through divine revelation.[66]

This 'humanistic' character of wisdom is particularly clear in the early usage of the term to indicate the skill of the soldier,[67] of a technician,[68] of a magician[69] or of an administrator.[70]

It is the faculty of cleverness, shrewdness, prudence, acute observation in the ordinary events of life, the result being embodied in some terse, striking, and not seldom witty saying. The word חָכְמָה becomes specially used of ethical and moral principles, that higher and finer prudence in the religious affairs of the man striving to harmonize his life with the law of God.[71]

---

65   von Rad, op. cit., p. 434.
66   Zimmerli, op. cit., pp. 190-91.
67   Isa. 10:13.
68   Exod. 28:3; 35:25; I Kings 7:14; Isa. 40:20.
69   Exod. 7:11.
70   Gen. 41:33, 39; Deut. 1:13; 16:19; 34:9.
71   Ranston, op. cit., p. 14.

Sub-Functions

If Hebrew proverbs resemble others in their philosophical function, they also are similar in some of their sub-functions. We frequently encounter humor and references to legal matters. And of course the function of ethical instruction looms largest. We shall discuss each of these secondary functions in turn.

Entertainment

Speaking of the biblical wisdom books, W.J. Beecher wrote in 1896: "They are remarkably rich in humor, though this is a fact which most readers fail to appreciate, by reason of our accustomed solemn way of looking at everything in the Bible."[72] The following examples make the point:

> Like a gold ring in a swine's snout
> is a beautiful woman without discretion.[73]

> The sluggard buries his hand in the dish
> and will not bring it back to his mouth.[74]

> He who meddles in a quarrel not his own
> is like one who takes a passing dog by the ears.[75]

A second way in which proverbs may be said to function as entertainment is in their relationship to the riddle. Although riddles are rare in the Old Testament, one finds a riddle-like quality in those proverbs characterized by comparative parallelism. As von Rad has written, "The hearer, who is also thinking along with the speaker, tries to run ahead of the latter and disentangle the meaning from its figurative clothing." [76] He cites two examples:

> Clouds and winds without rain
> is a man who boasts of a gift he does not give.[77]

72 Beecher, *op cit.,* p. 119.
73 Prov. 11:22.
74 Prov. 19:24.
75 Prov. 26:17.
76 von Rad, *op. cit.*, p. 423.
77 Prov. 25:14.

Like a dog that returns to its vomit
is a fool that repeats his folly.[77]

Some proverbs, in fact, may have originally circulated as riddles. [79]
For example, one can see how easily these proverbs could have
evolved:

Pleasant words are like a honeycomb,
sweetness to the soul and health to the body.[80]

Bread gained by deceit is sweet to a man,
but afterwards his mouth will be full of gravel.[81]

A good name is to be chosen rather than great riches,
and favor is better than silver or gold.[82]

Here we may well have original riddles combined with their answers
into proverbs, the questions being these: "What are pleasant like a
honeycomb, giving sweetness to the soul and health to the body?"
"What is at first sweet to man, but later is like a mouth full of
gravel?" "What is better than great riches?" "What is better than silver
or gold?"

The numerical proverbs may also have originally been transmitted
as riddles. [83] We can easily imagine the form that each would have
taken: "What four things are never satisfied?" And the answer would
follow: "Sheol, a barren womb, the earth ever thirsty for water, and
the fire which never says, 'Enough'." [84] Such riddles would have been
admirably suited for the instruction of the young, and may indeed
have been so used.

Gemser has made the interesting suggestion that the wise men
generally transmitted just one line of proverbial material, and it would
have been the exercise of students to build upon it. Sometimes, there-

78   Prov. 26:11.
79   Cheyne, *op. cit.*, p. 127; Elmslie, *op. cit .*, p. 51.
80   Prov. 16:24.
81   Prov. 20:17.
82   Prov. 22:1.
83   W.T. Davison, *The Wisdom-Literature of the Old Testament* (London:
Charles H. Kelly, 1894), p. 124; Eissfeldt, *op. cit.*, pp. 114-15; Gemser, *op. cit .*,
p. 3; Kent, *op. cit.*, p. 35.
84   Prov. 30:15-16.

fore, we can see two similar or identical first lines with variant second lines. In Prov. 10:1 and 15:20, for example, we have this line: "A wise son makes a glad father . . . . " But the concluding lines vary, 10:1 reading, " . . . but a foolish son is a sorrow to his mother". And in 15:20 we have, " . . . but a foolish man despises his mother". Sometimes it is the second lines which are alike, with the variations occurring in the first.[85]

Legal Usage

That there is a connection between proverbs and legal practice is quite clear. Both Gemser and Baumgartner have pointed this out, even noting the similarity to the legal use of proverbs in Africa.[86] We see in I Kings 12:10-11 the counsel for an executive decree couched in the form of proverbial speech:

> My little finger is thicker than my father's loins. And now, whereas my father laid upon you a heavy yoke, I will add to your yoke. My father chastised you with whips, but I will chastise you with scorpions.

Then, in verse 14, the royal decision is given in accordance with this counsel. In II Sam. 20:18 we see Joab deciding to spare Abel of Bethmaacah upon the citation of a proverb by a wise woman of the city: "Let them but ask counsel at Abel." [87]

Furthermore, it seems most likely that legal maxims were sometimes derived from proverbial sayings. In Exodus 23:8, for example, we read, "And you shall take no bribe, for a bribe blinds the officials, and subverts the cause of those who are in the right." And in Deut. 16:19 we read, "You shall not pervert justice; you shall not show partiality; and you shall not take a bribe, for a bribe blinds the eyes of the wise [who are sitting in judgment?] and subverts the cause of the righteous." Behind these ordinances perhaps stand such proverbs as these:

---

85 Prov. 10:2; 11:4; Gemser, *op. cit.*, p. 84.
86 Walter Baumgartner, "Die israelitische Weisheitsliteratur", *Theologische Rundschau*, Vol. V (1933), p. 284; Gemser, *op. cit.*, p. 2.
87 Baumgartner, *op. cit.*, p. 284.

A wicked man accepts a bribe from the bosom
to pervert the ways of justice.[88]

He who is greedy for unjust gain makes trouble for his house-
hold,
but he who hates bribes will live.[89]

The commandment against bearing false witness is at least adumbrated
in Proverbs 6:19 where, as one of the "six things which the LORD
hates" is "a false witness who breathes out lies". In Deut. 25:13-16
we find the following injuction: "You shall not have in your bag two
kinds of weights, a large and a small. A full and just weight you shall
have, a full and just measure you shall have; that your days may be
prolonged in the land which the LORD your God gives you." And in
Prov. 1:11 we read,

A false balance is an abomination to the LORD,
but a just weight is his delight.

And Prov. 20:10 reads as follows:

Diverse weights and diverse measures
are both alike an abomination to the LORD.

Or verse 23 of the same chapter says,

Diverse weights are an abomination to the LORD,
and false scales are not good.

Deut. 19:14 says that " . . . you shall not remove your neighbor's
landmark, which the men of old have set". And in Deut. 27:17 the
landmark remover is among those who are cursed. A parallel is found
in Prov. 22:28:

Remove not the ancient landmark
which your fathers have set.

88   Prov. 17:23.
89   Prov. 15:27.

In Prov. 23:10 we have another parallel:

> Do not remove an ancient landmark
> or enter the fields of the fatherless.[90]

It may be objected here that the priority of the proverbial material cannot be assumed. But if we look at evidence from ancient Egypt and Babylonia this priority seems most likely. With regard to bribery, we read in the *Instruction of Amenemopet*,

> Do not accept the bribe of a powerful man,
> Nor oppress for him the disabled.[91]

As for false witness, we have in the same work these words:

> Do not bear witness with false words,
> Nor support another person (*thus*) with thy tongue.[92]

Honest weights and measures are enjoined in a Babylonian preceptive hymn:

> The merchant who [practices] trickery as he holds the balances,
> Who uses two sets of weights, thus lowering the . . . . . ,
> He is disappointed in the matter of profit and loses [his capital].

> The honest merchant who holds the balances [and gives] good weight —
> Everything is presented to him in good measure [. . .]

> The merchant who practices trickery as he holds the cord measure,
> Who weighs out loans (or corn) by the minimum standard, but requires a large quantity in repayment,
> The curse of the people will overtake him before his time,
> . . . . [93]

---

90 For a discussion of the probable reason for the use of wisdom material in Deuteronomy 25:13-16 and 19:14 see C.M. Carmichael, "Deuteronomic Laws, Wisdom, and Historical Traditions", *Journal of Semitic Studies*, Vol. XXII (Autumn, 1967), pp. 198-206.

91 Pritchard, *Texts*, p. 424.

92 *Op. cit.*, p. 423.

93 Lambert, *op. cit.*, p. 133.

And Van Dijk notes that among those whom the goddess Nanshe hates, according to a Sumerian wisdom text, are "those who substitute the small weight for the large, who substitute the small measure for the large". [94] In the *Instruction of Amenemopet* we have this advice:

> Do not lean on the scales nor falsify the weights,
> Nor damage the fractions of the measure. [95]

The proverbs concerned with removing the ancient landmark are widely believed to be more directly dependent upon Amenemopet:

> Do not carry off the landmark at the boundaries of the arable land,
> Nor disturb the position of the measuring cord;
> Be not greedy after a cubit of land,
> Nor encroach upon the boundaries of a widow. [96]

Finally, there are several proverbs which deal with what we might call 'legal morality'. Prov. 17:15 is a typical example:

> He who justifies the wicked and he who condemns the righteous
> are both alike an abomination to the LORD. [97]

We shall have occasion in Chapter 4 to note what appears to be a further influence of the proverb upon Israel's legal material.

 ## Instruction

The most obvious secondary function of proverbs in Israel is clearly that of the instruction of youth. The recurrent phrase, "my son", so typical of Near Eastern wisdom, points to this usage. The most obvious indication of Proverbs' use in teaching is to be seen in its content, and needs little elaboration. Throughout the book of Proverbs

94 Van Dijk, *op. cit.*, p. 114.
95 Pritchard, *Texts*, p. 423.
96 *Op. cit.*, p. 422. See Oesterley, *op. cit.*, p. 1 (= 50). A succinct argument for the dependence of Deuteronomy upon wisdom material is seen in M. Weinfeld, "The Origin of the Humanism in Deuteronomy", *Journal of Biblical Literature*, Vol. LXXX (September, 1961), pp. 241-47.
97 See also 18:5; 22:23-26; 25:8-10.

the 'advice-to-young-men' motif is loud and clear. The youngster is cautioned against the wiles of the adulteress, admonished to hold his tongue, pay diligent attention to wisdom's teachings, deal honestly with his fellow men, and avoid association with the wicked. And if it is true that many of the parallel forms derived from the practice of the student responding appropriately to quotations given by the teacher, then this also would point to instructional use.

We have no direct evidence of wisdom schools in ancient Israel, but yet considerable indirect evidence can be cited, especially if we can identify the wise man and the scribe. And this identification, it seems, is not unjustified. [98] Although Ranston affirmed that there was a clear distinction between the ancient scribe and the wise man, and that the two were not to be identified until the time of Ben Sira, he yet admitted that most wise men were probably also scribes. He did believe, though, that not all scribes were wise men. [99] At any rate the two probably moved in the same circles and had much of their education in common. In Jeremiah 8:8-9, for example, the two groups seem to be identified. Furthermore, the wisdom of ancient Babylonia and Egypt is largely the concern of the scribal class. If it is objected that the form of proverbs points to oral transmission rather than written, we may note the use of proverbs for the teaching of writing in both Egypt and Sumer. [100]

Like other cultures, Israel seems to have employed her scribes in important government positions. We read in II Sam. 8:16-17, with reference to David's administration, that "Jehoshaphat the son of Ahilud was recorder" and that "Seraiah was secretary". In 20:25 we note again that Jehoshaphat was recorder, "and Sheva was secretary". In Solomon's time, according to I Kings 4:3, among the officials "Elihoreph and Ahijah the sons of Shisha were secretaries". Later we are told that Shebna was secretary under Hezekiah; [101] Shaphan

---

98   Fritsch, "Proverbs . . .", p. 769; Hugo Gressmann, *Israels Spruchweisheit im Zusammenhang der Weltliteratur* (Berlin: Karl Curtius, 1925), pp. 47-49; J. Coert Rylaarsdam, *Revelation in Jewish Wisdom Literature* (Chicago: The University of Chicago Press, 1946), p. 9.

99   Ranston, *op. cit.,* p. 13.

100 Gemser, *op. cit.,* p. 3.

101 II Kings 19:2.

served as secretary under Josiah, [102] and Elishama was Jehoiakim's secretary. [103]

It would seem that with the establishment of the monarchy, and particularly during the reign of Solomon, there will have been a crying need for scribes in Israel. Not only would the extensive domestic programs of Solomon have necessitated the employment of men who could read and write; but his foreign connections would have demanded them also, even men who understood more than one language. [104] Sometimes foreign scribes may have been employed in royal service, or Israelite scribes may have been educated abroad. "An dem Königshof Salomos und seiner Nachfolger waren ausländische oder im Ausland gebildete Schreiber als höhere Beamte, Diplomaten usw. unentbehrlich . . . Dort fand Weisheit ihre erste Plegestätte . . ." [105] Hezekiah's Shebna may have been a foreigner. [106] Such a highly developed state as Solomon's is simply unthinkable without a considerable force of educated administrators and secretaries. And since Solomon has traditionally been closely associated with the wisdom movement, it is hardly to be doubted that the sage-scribe rose to prominence during his reign. [107] As Noth has written,

---

102 II Kings 22:3.

103 Jer. 36:9-10. One wishes that the Hebrew terms were more precise here. The word 'secretary' (בֹּפֵר, בֹּוזֵר) probably corresponds to the Akkadian *seperu*, 'scribe' (so Montgomery); but while the term is commonly taken, as it is used here, to mean 'state official', the exact nature of the position designated is something of a mystery. The term 'recorder' (מַזְכִּיר) is also not entirely clear, but it undoubtedly also refers to some sort of state functionary – 'remembrancer' perhaps, as several have suggested (The word is a hiph. form of זָכַר , 'remember'). Or perhaps it refers to a high court office or a kind of 'prosecuting attorney'. See Brevard S. Childs, *Memory and Tradition in Israel* (=*Studies in Biblical Theology*, No. 37) (London: SCM Press, 1962). That both terms refer to literate bureaucrats, however, is hardly to be doubted; and as such they refer to members of the intelligentsia who will have been the conservators of wisdom.

104 Bentzen, *op. cit.*, RM Vol. I, p. 171.

105 Ernst Würthwein, *Die Weisheit Ägyptens und das Alte Testament* (Marburg: N.G. Elwert, 1960), p. 4. See also Oesterley, *op. cit.*, p. 103.

106 Francis L. Griffith, "The Teaching of Amenophis, the Son of Kanekht", *Journal of Egyptian Archaeology*, Vol. XII (1926), p. 231.

107 R.B.Y. Scott has pointed out that the biblical evidence for Solomon's connection with wisdom is late and legendary, and he argues for Hezekiah's

From the earliest times in the ancient Orient the 'wisdom' literature has promoted the transmission of a body of knowledge and experience within a 'cultured' stratum represented, above all, by the 'learned' scribes in the great cultures of the ancient Orient. Solomon's 'wisdom' is explicitly related to the great 'wisdom' tradition of the ancient Orient . . . [108]

Given this great demand for administrators in Solomon's time and afterwards, it is reasonable to assume that schools for scribal training existed in Israel, and that it was under their auspices that the proverb was cultivated. As Kittel has written,

Schreibkunst und Beamtentum forderte Schulen und Unterweisung der Jugend. Die beste Methode der Underweisung aber schien die durch den bildhaften, in Vergleichen und Rätselworten sich ergehenden und in die leicht fassliche Form der Versrede gekleideten Sinnspruch des Vaters an den Sohn zu sein.[109]

Whether these schools were related to Canaanite prototypes or were modeled after Babylonian and Egyptian institutions we have no way of knowing. But there is some small evidence from ancient Shechem that children were sometimes sent away from home for an education, and this practice may have been continued by the later Hebrews. Our evidence is in the form of a letter sent apparently by a teacher in a city at some remove to a noble at Shechem, complaining that anticipated tuition fees have not been forthcoming. [110] In support of the theory that the writer is, in fact, a school master or school mistress, we note the opinion of Albright:

---

reign as the time when Egyptian wisdom made its most significant impression upon Israel. See his "Solomon and the Beginning of Wisdom in Israel", *Wisdom in Israel and in the Ancient Near East*, eds. H.H. Rowley, Martin Noth, D. Winton Thomas (= Supplements to *Vetus Testamentum*, Vol. III) (Leiden: E.J. Brill, 1960), pp. 262-79. Probably there was a significant impact during Hezekiah's reign; but, as Scott himself admits, "general historical considerations do not preclude, but rather favor, the connection with Solomon of the origins of literary wisdom in Israel". *Op. cit.*, p. 279.

108   Martin Noth, *The History of Israel*, 2d. ed., translation rev. by P.R. Ackroyd (New York: Harper & Brothers, 1960), pp. 218-19.

109   Rudolph Kittel, *Geschichte des Volkes Israel*, Vol. III (Stuttgart: W. Kohlhammer, 1929), p. 716.

110   Pritchard, *Texts*, p. 490.

In general both script and language are superior, which would be easy to understand if the writer of the letter were a man who headed a school for future cuneiform scribes. That the writer had pupils from other sources appears to follow from the fact that cessation of tuition fees in the case of Birashshena did not force her (or him) to stop teaching.[111]

We also read of a city called Keriath-sepher in Josh. 15:15, and this might possibly have been a training city for scribes.[112] At any rate, the existence of such schools is practically a logical necessity. The scribal school was already an ancient institution by the time of Solomon, and had probably been using proverbs in its instruction from as early as the third millenium B.C. To assume any markedly different situation within Israel, especially in light of the biblical allusions and the obviously pedagogical tone of Proverbs, would be to run counter to all existing evidence.[113]

EXTENDED USAGE

So much for our general discussion of ancient Israel's proverbs. It remains to be seen how this form was utilized by later generations in those books which now constitute our Old Testament and Apocrypha.

The principal use of the material, of course, was made by those who stood as the immediate heirs of the wisdom tradition: the sages of post-monarchic Israel. From their hands came Proverbs, Ecclesiastes, Job and the Apocryphal works of Ecclesiasticus and the Wisdom of Solomon, each treating in its own particular way this most basic form.

Proverbs

It goes without saying that no one would argue seriously today in favor of the Solomonic authorship of the entire book of Proverbs.

111   William Foxwell Albright, "A Teacher to a Man of Shechem About 1400 B.C.", *Bulletin of the American Schools of Oriental Research*, No. 86 (April, 1942), p. 31.
112   Gemser, *op. cit.*, p. 2.
113   A recent work that stresses the importance of the school in Israel is Hermisson, *op. cit.*.

Some, however, would affirm the possible presence of his kingly wit in 10:1-22:16, specifically labeled as his work and generally believed to be the earliest collection in the book. Certainly such a possibility exists; but with the extreme difficulty of dating the proverb, and with Solomon's glorification as Israel's wise man par excellence, all conclusions regarding his authorship of anything in the book appear to be highly subjective.

The book itself is made up of a number of separate collections, each having its own characteristics and its own peculiar history. Division I (1:1-19:18) has generally been felt to be the most recent, exhibiting as it does the more expanded essay form not found in the rest of the book. Furthermore, the personification of wisdom, found here, has widely been assumed to have a Greek provenance. Albright, however, followed by Fritsch, would date chapters 8 and 9 among the oldest sections of the book, citing in them extensive Phoenician and Ugaritic influence. [114] And, in fact, the case for Greek influence has been weakened considerably in recent years.

This material is of interest here, however, not because of matters of date, but rather because we see in it the use of the basic proverbial distich in what Oesterley has termed "short sections approximating to a miniature essay form". [115] The writer has linked the typical distichs together in logical sequences, giving the appearance of a more narrative style and pointing perhaps to the more unified verse structure seen in the poetic material of Job. [116] Is this, then, a kind of 'transitional' material revealing a stage in the growing sophistication of poetic art? It would be tempting to think so, but much more evidence is wanted.

Division II, "The Proverbs of Solomon" (10:1-22:16), is composed of 375 proverbs, each comprised of the typical balanced, parallel form, with the exception of 19:7, which contains three stichs. There is a concentration of antithetical parallel forms in chapters 10-15, the remainder presenting a more varied picture. Practically no principle of

---

114   Albright, "Some Canaanite . . .", pp. 7-9; Fritsch, "The Book . . .", p. 767; R.N. Whybray, *Wisdom in Proverbs* (= *Studies in Biblical Theology*, No. 45) (London: SCM Press, 1965), p. 106.
115   Oesterley, *op. cit.*, p. xiii.
116   Toy, *op. cit.*, p. xxviii.

arrangement is to be noted here. And certainly we observe nothing at all akin to the essay-units of chapters 1-9.

Division III (22:17-24:34) is composed of several smaller collections, and the material in 22:17-23:14 displays clear literary dependence upon the *Instruction of Amenemopet*. Discrete parallel types are not so frequent as in 10:1-22:16, and the direct second person injunction appears often, particularly in the verses dependent upon Amenemopet. One also observes some clustering of proverbs into larger units, reminiscent of Division I.

Division IV (25:1-29:27) purports to contain additional proverbs of Solomon "which the men of Hezekiah copied". [117] Here we find parallelism used extensively, particularly the antithetic type, recalling to mind chapters 10-15. We also find in this section the use of the comparative form, already discussed. [118]

Divisions V, VI and VII bring the book to a close, and contain what were probably originally several independent collections. Here it is that we have the skeptical words of Agur (30:1ff.), the numerical proverbs, [119] the "words of Lemuel" (31:1ff.) and the concluding acrostic poem in praise of the good housewife, called by Pfeiffer "by far the best acrostic alphabetic poem in the Old Testament". [120] The familiar parallel forms are to be found here, but they are not nearly so distinct and plentiful as in 10:1-22:16. And again we find a kind of 'miniature essay form', most notable in 30:1ff. and in the concluding poem (31:10-31).

Ecclesiastes

The book of Ecclesiastes, composed probably during the third century B.C., contains a great deal of material which differs from the simple parallel construction of the typical Hebrew proverb. But still much of the old flavor lingers on: statements expressed in two parallel halves, comparative forms of the 'Better is A than B' variety, direct second per-

117   Prov. 25:1.
118   Above, p. 61.
119   Above, p. 62.
120   Pfeiffer, *op. cit.*, p. 645.

son exhortations, the various types of parallelism, rhyme and wordplays. But in addition to these familiar features we find also in Ecclesiastes the use of other forms: the rhetorical question, multiple-line forms, extended observations along a unified theme, and the use of the first person statement ("I saw..."), resulting in a general loosening of parallelism and thereby approaching to a prose style.[121]

It is of especial significance here, however, to make note of Koheleth's use of proverbs, "kurze, knappe Sprüche, die nicht nur in ihrer Form, sondern auch im Inhalt stark an die Proverbien gemahnen". [122] For it is perhaps in his employment of proverbs, especially of the balanced, parallel variety, that his membership in the community of sages is most apparent. The following examples might just as well come from Proverbs:

> The words of a wise man's mouth win him favor,
> but the lips of a fool consume him.[123]

> A wise man's heart inclines him toward the right,
> but a fool's heart toward the left.[124]

Some scholars, to be sure, have seen most of these proverbs as the glosses of a pious orthodoxy inserted to make our Preacher more acceptable to conventional Judaism. These scholars have been unable to account for the inconsistencies of thought represented by Koheleth's skeptical pronouncements on the one hand and his traditional proverbial material on the other, particularly those aphorisms of 9:17-10:20, reminiscent of Proverbs with regard to both form and content.[125]

---

121 Walther Zimmerli, *Das Buch des Predigers Salomo* (*Das Alte Testament Deutsch*, Teilband 16/I) (Göttingen: Vandenhoeck und Ruprecht, 1962), pp. 128-30. We are here simply speaking of the character of Ecclesiastes, and not suggesting any uniqueness of style on his part. A comparison with the wisdom of Egypt and Babylonia would expose the dubiety of any such claim.

122 Walther Zimmerli, *Die Weisheit des Predigers Salomo* (*Aus der Welt der Religion*) (Berlin: Verlag von Alfred Töpelmann, 1936), p. 12.

123 Eccles. 10:12.

124 Eccles. 10:2.

125 See, for example, Morris Jastrow, *A Gentle Cynic, Being a Translation of the Book of Koheleth Commonly Known as Ecclestiastes, Stripped of Later Additions; Also Its Origin, Growth and Interpretation* (Philadelphia: J.B.

In more recent years, however, Ecclesiastes has been taken as much more of a unity, and the proverbs have not so frequently been denied to the original author. [126] There are several reasons why we may see many, if not most, of them as comprising a part of the original work. First, of course, they are sometimes integrally related to their surrounding material; they may state a conclusion, [127] serve as a foil for argument, support an argument, or serve as a kind of 'text' for further discussion. [128] But a second argument can be put forth, applying particularly to those proverbs which seem inconsistent with the main lines of Koheleth's thought. We shall see in Chapter 5 that from ancient times the optimistic, prudential type of wisdom has existed side by side with its more skeptical counterpart. Both types are, in fact, to be seen in Proverbs, and it should not surprise us to find both varieties present here. We know, furthermore, from our study of Proverbs that the aphorism need not agree with its neighbor in order to be perceived as 'true'. Just as the aphorist could put together Prov. 26:4-5, so could Koheleth put in juxtaposition concise, summary and contradictory statements which were true in his own life. As Bentzen has written, "The aphoristic form of the book warns us to be cautious in drawing too far-reaching conclusions from apparent contradictions." [129] Koheleth, we believe, knew from his own experience the value of prudence and 'right living'; he knew that "it is better for a man to hear the rebuke of the wise than to hear the song of fools". [130] But he also knew that man was limited, that he could not

---

Lippincott Company, 1919), pp. 76-86; George Aaron Barton, *A Critical and Exegetical Commentary on the Book of Ecclesiastes* (*The International Critical Commentary*) (New York: Charles Scribner's Sons, 1909), p. 46.

126 The whole matter of the integrity of Ecclesiastes is a complex and much debated one. For a discussion of varying views see O.S. Rankin, "The Book of Ecclesiastes, Introduction and Exegesis", *The Interpreter's Bible*, Vol. V, pp. 7-12; Walter Baumgartner, "The Wisdom Literature", *The Old Testament and Modern Study*, ed. H.H. Rowley (Oxford: At the Clarendon Press, 1951), pp. 222-24.

127 Hans Wilhelm Hertzberg, *Der Prediger* (*Kommentar zum Alten Testament* Vol. XVII, Part 4) (Gütersloher Verlagshaus Gerd Mohn, 1963), p. 30.

128 Robert Gordis, *Koheleth – The Man and His World*, 2d augmented ed. (New York: Bloch Publishing Company for the Jewish Theological Seminary of America, 1955), pp. 96-105.

129 Bentzen, *op. cit.*, Vol. II, p. 191.

130 Eccles. 7:5.

fathom the mysteries of God's dealings with his children nor escape, however wise, his inevitable death. "For the wise man as of the fool there is no enduring remembrance, seeing that in the days to come all will have been long forgotten. How the wise man dies just like the fool!" [131] He has spoken to us with candor, and if his words are inconsistent, then it is because he has spoken from the depths of his inconsistent being and not from detached and systematic 'philosophizing'. Koheleth was, in fine, more of a poet than a metaphysician.

A third reason to doubt that the so-called 'orthodox' proverbs are later additions has to do with the relatively short period of time between the book's composition and its attaining to canonical status. It has been suggested that there simply would not have been enough time for such additions to have become incorporated into the text. [132]

And finally, it is difficult to see how any interpolator would be content with his doctored product if the original was so distasteful; one would expect him, rather, to have moved for the book's suppression. And if it was the popularity of the book which prevented its suppression, then it is difficult to believe that the altered version could have succeeded in supplanting the popular original.

Job

The Book of Job is unique in the Old Testament, and its form defies all classification.

It falls into no recognized class of literature. It is a poem, or a series of poems, and it is a dialogue, but we can say no more. It is too long for a lyric, and though it is full of intense emotion, even of passion, it scarcely comes into that category. It is hardly a drama, for there surely must be some kind of action in dramatic poetry . . . It might be a philosophical dialogue, but there is more feeling in it than reasoned argument . . . The book is *sui generis*; all we can say of it is that it is the Book of Job. [133]

---

131   Eccles. 2:16.
132   Hertzberg, *op. cit.*, p. 41.
133   Theodore H. Robinson, *Job and His Friends* (London: SCM Press Ltd., 1954), p. 36.

Much of the poetic structure, however, is similar to that of Proverbs. We find synonymous, antithetic and synthetic parallelism;[134] and assonance is employed freely.[135] But such devices are characteristic of Hebrew poetry in general, and unless we are to attribute the origin of such forms and devices to the ancient proverb makers,[136] we are not justified in establishing proverbs' influence here.[137]

It does seem, though, that a number of proverbs have been used in the poem; and they appear to bear the mark of the professional aphorist. Since they are not so frequently noted,[138] a number of examples are here cited:

Can mortal man be righteous before God?
    can a man be pure before his Maker?[139]

For affliction does not come from the dust,
    nor does trouble sprout from the ground.[140]

Does the wild ass bray when he has grass,
    or the ox low over his fodder?[141]

As the cloud fades and vanishes,
    so he who goes down to Sheol does not come up.[142]

But a stupid man will get understanding
    when a wild ass's colt is born a man.[143]

Drought and heat snatch away the snow waters;
    so does Sheol those who have sinned.[144]

134   Samuel Terrien, "The Book of Job, Introduction and Exegesis", *The Interpreter's Bible*, Vol. III, p. 892.
135   William Barron Stevenson, *The Poem of Job, a Literary Study With a New Translation (The Schweich Lectures of the British Academy,* 1943) (London: Oxford University Press, 1947), p. 60.
136   Below, pp. 92-93.
137   Note, however, the numerical form of 5:17ff.
138   But see Pfeiffer, *op. cit.*, p. 685; Terrien, "The Book . . .", pp. 952-53, 995.
139   Job 4:17.
140   Job 5:6.
141   Job 6:5.
142   Job. 7:9.
143   Job 11:12.
144   Job 24:19.

The Book of Job is always classified as wisdom literature, largely because of its content. [145] The propriety of this classification is, however, made even more obvious when the inclusion of proverbs is noted. Whether the poet utilized existing proverbs in the instances cited, or whether he merely adopted the proverb form, his debt to the aphorist is plain.

Ecclesiasticus

In Sirach we come closer to the form of our canonical Proverbs than in any other work from the period. Writing early in the second century B.C., Sirach uses most of the familiar forms and devices from Hebrew proverbs: synonymous, antithetic, synthetic parallelism; comparative forms; second person injunctions and prohibitions; metaphor and simile. Even the numerical form found in Proverbs, Job, Amos and Ugaritic literature is used at several points: 23:16-17; 25:7-11; 26:5-6, 28; 50:25-26. [146]

Ecclesiasticus differs from Proverbs, however, in that it rarely displays isolated proverbs, preferring instead to join them one to another as verses in larger units. "Sirach strings his pearls together, hardly ever mounting them individually." [147]

That the proverb continued to play an important part in the circles of the wise we know from Sirach's own words. He disparages manual laborers, necessary though they are, because "they are not found using proverbs". [148] And conversely, he praises the student of law who "will seek out the hidden meanings of proverbs". [149] He advises his readers, moreover, not to "let wise proverbs escape you". [150] And he tells us that among the sages of his time, "Those who understand sayings become skilled themselves, and pour forth apt proverbs". [151]

---

145   Samuel Rolles Driver and George Buchanan Gray, *A Critical and Exegetical Commentary on the Book of Job*, Vol. I (The International Critical Commentary) (New York: Charles Scribner's Sons, 1921), pp. xxi-xxii.
146   For a brief discussion of some of these and other characteristic forms see Robert H. Pfeiffer, *History of New Testament Times with an Introduction to the Apocrypha* (New York: Harper & Brothers Publishers, 1949), pp. 402-403.
147   *Op cit.*, p. 402.
148   Ecclus. 38:33.
149   Ecclus. 39:3.
150   Ecclus. 6:35.
151   Ecclus. 18:29.

The Wisdom of Solomon

Perhaps the furthest departure from the style of Hebrew proverbs is to be found in the Wisdom of Solomon, composed toward the beginning of the Christian Era. Not only does the author launch into the flowing forms of an address or exhortation, but he weaves into the texture of his writing those stylistic features which are peculiarly Greek: sorites, syncrisis, definition, catalogues.[152]

Yet characteristic Hebrew forms are not lacking.[153] Synonymous, antithetic and synthetic parallelism are there, especially in the first five chapters.[154] Among the several Hebrew features which have interest for us, however, the proverb demands the most attention. For even in this work the homely maxim makes its appearance, and so bears witness — feeble though it may be — to the book's aphoristic heritage. The following examples, most of them noted by Pfeiffer,[155] are to the point:

> For perverse thoughts separate men from God,
> and when his power is tested, it convicts the foolish.[156]

> For the fruit of good labors is renowned,
> and the root of understanding does not fail.[157]

> But children of adulterers will not come to maturity,
> and the offspring of an unlawful union will perish.[158]

> but understanding is gray hair for men,
> and a blameless life is ripe old age.[159]

> For the lowliest man may be pardoned in mercy,
> but mighty men will be mightily tested.[160]

> A multitude of wise men is the salvation of the world,
> and a sensible king is the stability of his people.[161]

---

152 Pfeiffer, *History* . . . , pp. 329-31.
153 They derive, however, from the Greek rather than the Hebrew Bible. See Pfeiffer, *History* . . . , p. 331.
154 Ibid.; Eissfeldt, *Einleitung* . . . , p. 813.
155 Pfeiffer, *History* . . . , p. 330.
156 Wisd. of Sol. 1:3.
157 Wisd. of Sol. 3:15.
158 Wisd. of Sol. 3:16.
159 Wisd. of Sol. 4:9.
160 Wisd. of Sol. 6:6.
161 Wisd. of Sol. 6:24.

COMPARISONS

Ancient Near Eastern Proverbs and Proverbs in General

From our study this far it has become clear that the proverb was a universal phenomenon in the ancient Near East as it is in our world. Both as to function and form, these ancient precepts correspond to what we know of the proverb in general: They are short, easy to remember, frequently poetic, and constitute a kind of 'primitive philosophy'. Furthermore, they find application in instruction, as do those of primitive societies in our own time; they seem to bear a close relation to law in ancient Hebrew culture, as they do in Western tradition and in primitive communities; and they sometimes serve to provide entertainment to the teller and the hearer, as do many proverbs everywhere.

Among the notable features seen in these ancient Near Eastern maxims and elsewhere, one seems to have particular significance. We have noted Gemser's suggestion that the Hebrew parallel proverbs developed by a kind of 'riddle game' in which the first stich was answered by a corresponding second. [162] Kelso, we saw, reported that a similar practice was common among the Chinese;[163] and Loeb discussed the same phenomenon occurring among the African Kuanyama. [164] More recently J.C. Messenger has reported this same phenomenon as a feature of Anang culture in south-eastern Nigeria. He reports that these people use the proverb-riddle (as he terms it) in instruction, although the fun comes not in the challenge of matching, but in providing the proper learned response. If a man has made up such a proverb-riddle he will immediately tell the response instead of depending upon his colleagues to create a corresponding reply. Quite frequently, Messenger says, an individual will propose a proverb to a group, and the group will then respond with the proper matching proverb. Or sometimes a proverb will be given by one individual to another as a form of greeting, the greeting to be returned by the corresponding response. Messenger's examples of the proverb-pairs which are so used are unfortunately too culture-bound to be clear

---

162   Above, pp. 75-76.
163   Above, p. 32.
164   Above, p. 32.

without a detailed explanation. But they do reveal what we might call a synonymous parallel construction.[165]

The basic phenomenon of the proverb-riddle is highly suggestive of what might be the genesis of the parallel proverb in the ancient Near East, and perhaps of parallelism in general. Granting that only 'synonymous parallelism' is evident in the more contemporary examples, it would be quite natural for this to develop into the ancient variations which we have noted. This would, we think, help to explain the relationship between the popular one-line proverb and the cultivated parallel form. Schmidt believes that the simple, popular prose proverb was collected, redacted and given its parallel literary structure by the wise men.[166] If he is right, then the basic incorporating process may be similar to the 'proverb games' played in some primitive cultures of our own time. On the other hand it does not seem necessary, in light of our ethnological data, always to presuppose the endeavors of such a sophisticated elite. At any rate, the existence of a kind of synonymous parallelism resulting from primitive proverb matching seems certain. The following examples from the Kuanyama make this clear:

A long millet crop brings birds to the garden.
A long kraal entrance brings war to kraal.[167]

Although your small urine pot is good, you cannot eat from it.
Even if your sister is beautiful, you cannot have sexual inter-
course with her.[168]

If you climb an anthill you fall.
If you kill your mother you will have a hard time.[169]

Ancient Near Eastern Proverbs and the Proverbs of Israel

When we compare the ancient Hebrew proverb with the wisdom of the ancient Near East, the similarities are indeed striking. We find proverbs in Sumerian and Egyptian literature and strong hints of their usage in Canaan. In form we find many of them displaying syno-

---

165 J.C. Messenger, "Anang Proverb-Riddles", *Journal of American Folklore*, Vol. LXIII (July, 1960), pp. 225-235.
166 Schmidt, *op. cit.*, pp. 12-17.
167 Loeb, "Kuanyama . . .", p. 332.
168 *Op. cit.*, p. 333.
169 *Op. cit.*, p. 332.

nymous, antithetic, comparative and synthetic parallelism. They use simile, metaphor and assonance. They have been combined into the gnomic essay form, or what approaches this form.

Even some of the more unusual variations of Hebrew proverbs have their counterparts. The couplet of two synonymously parallel elements standing in comparative parallelism with a climactic second stich is similar to Sumerian usage. And, although not in proverb form, the same basic structure is observed in Canaanite literature. The 'Better is A than B' form is found in Egyptian wisdom. The form of the numerical proverb in which the introductory line states one number less than the total is paralleled in Canaanite literature. And the direct, second person moral injunction is found in both Babylonian and Egyptian wisdom, particularly the latter.[170]

Apart from their philosophical function the proverbs of Sumer, Egypt and Israel appear to have been used in education, both as writing exercises and as ethical instruction. Humor, while not generally present in Egyptian and Sumerian proverbs, plays a part in the Hebrew maxims. And we may suppose that many proverbs, while not blatantly mirth-provoking, did serve to entertain those who employed them (as with the proverb riddle). And while legal usage is not so obvious, there appears to be a strong connection between legal practice and certain proverbs in Israel. For the possibility that proverbs may have had a legal function in Egypt, see below, pp. 115-117.

Both the proverbs of Israel and those of their neighbors came to be used in a wider wisdom context, showing their importance for those sages who went beyond the mere collecting of maxims to the composition of extended treatises.

CONCLUSIONS

So far as form and function are concerned, Israel seems to have contributed little to the proverb lore of the ancient Near East. Her scribe sages, who promulgated the proverb and used it in their schools, stood in an international tradition already ancient by Solomon's time. And

---

170   For other similarities of form between Egyptian and Hebrew wisdom see Humbert, *op. cit.*, pp. 64-67.

consequently it is impossible to date Hebrew proverbs, however close-ly we may fix the time of their recording.[171]

Undoubtedly the people of Israel knew and used proverbs from the very earliest times, even though they may not have cultivated them extensively before the establishment of the monarchy. It is almost impossible to imagine how the Hebrews could have existed without being touched by this most universal form in circulation throughout the Near East for many hundreds of years before the time of Moses. Even the most poetic varieties of the learned scribes would surely have been known; with their compact, easy-to-remember and compelling form, it is hardly conceivable that they could have remained the ex-clusive property of the educated elite for so many centuries.

Therefore, to assert that Israel's wisdom is late and foreign, as has so often been done in the past, is to ignore a great amount of prover-bial evidence pointing in the opposite direction. In fact one can more legitimately argue that it was the very late and perhaps foreign (Kenite?) Yahwistic-nationalistic element which was added to the more indigenous wisdom tradition and which significantly modified it. It will be the task of Chapters 4 and 5 to discuss the place of wisdom and its proverbs in the context of later Hebraic faith.

---

[171] Robinson, *op. cit.*, p. 167.

4. PROVERBS AND ISRAEL'S RELIGION

It has been generally recognized that Israel's wisdom is not clearly connected to such theological themes as election, covenant and the historical traditions of the Hebrew community. And since biblical scholars generally have found the dominating factor of Israel's faith to be her sacred history, they have frequently regarded the wisdom literature as a late addendum to the religion of Israel and not truly characteristic of Hebraic thought. It now seems from our study of proverbs that this is an entirely too cavalier way of dealing with this body of material — or, better, of *not* dealing with it.

It is our intent in this chapter to indicate and examine some of the reasons for this shabby treatment of wisdom and to go on to suggest some basic connections between wisdom and other elements of the Hebrew Faith — all the while concentrating upon the role of proverbs in shedding light on the problem.

We have already indicated several possible reasons for the eclipse of our book of Proverbs, and we have suggested that Proverbs' fate was closely connected to that of the biblical wisdom literature in general. And now, as we turn to the reasons for wisdom's being pushed to the sidelines, three stand forth as significant.

The first reason would seem to be the fact that only three of our thirty-nine Old Testament books, as most Protestant scholars classify them, can be termed 'wisdom literature'. And one may suspect that this one-sided ratio has frequently led to the facile conclusion that the wisdom material was roughly only one thirteenth as significant as the traditions out of which most of the other books evolved! But obviously any argument based upon such an assumption is empty on its face. Just as so much ancient Hebrew literature has not survived, one may suspect that a rather considerable amount of wisdom literature, for one reason or another, has passed into oblivion. And who is to say, on

the basis of what has remained, whether it might not even have domi-
nated Israel's thought at some point of her history? It may well never
have done so, but the issue is not to be decided by counting books and
figuring percentages. And one must always remember that in comparison to the wise men of the Old Testament, "the prophets and priests
were by far the more prominent, since Israel's history was written
from both a priestly and prophetic point of view".[1]

But a second reason has also had its effect, and it seems to run
something like this: Hebrew thought is active, concrete and non-speculative. Wisdom, however, is clearly speculative. Therefore wisdom is
not Hebrew. Some of us, this writer included, have sought to avoid
embarrassment by stating that Hebrew thought, with the exception of
the wisdom tradition, was active, concrete and non-speculative. This,
however, is tantamount to saying that Hebrew thought, apart from
her speculative thought, was non-speculative. And one suspects that
perhaps the qualification is not very helpful.

As for the assumption itself, that Israel was not given to speculative
thinking, one may conjecture that it has grown out of two highly
questionable theses. The first one would claim that primitive peoples
in general simply are incapable of thinking speculatively; and so Israel,
during the time of her primitive beginnings, cannot be assumed to
have been any different in this regard. Johannes Pederson, so profoundly steeped in anthropological research, appears to reflect this
orientation when he writes as follows:

The soul can not, as long as it is a soul, desist from being a committed
whole, characterized by volitions and action. Therefore the Israelite
manner of *thinking* is of a different kind from ours. What we call
objective, that is to say inactive, theoretical thinking without further
implications, does not exist in the case of the Israelite.[2]

We cannot help but see the ancient proverb as giving the lie to such a
view. And more recent anthropological study, as we have seen, argues
tellingly in the opposite direction.[3]

---

1   Fritsch, "The Book . . . ", p. 769.
2   Johannes Pedersen, *Israel: Its Life and Culture,* Vols. I-II (London: Oxford
University Press, 1926), p. 106.
3   Above, pp. 28-31. See also Childs, *op. cit.,* pp. 17-30.

The second thesis is based upon a linguistic argument in which it is proposed that the Hebrew language reflects a totalistic, concrete, active, non-speculative way of thinking contrasting sharply with the more static, analytic speculative thought of the Greeks. Once again, the existence of the proverb in Israel constitutes no small embarrassment to such a view. Furthermore, the work of James Barr on biblical semantics constitutes a devastating attack against it.[4]

Apart from these two theses one may also surmise that the zeal of the *Heilsgeschichte* theologians has led to the kind of oversimplification which looks at ancient Hebrew culture from one point of view only, and quietly ignores the presence of wisdom in Israel or blithely dismisses it as un-Hebrew activity.

A third reason for seeing wisdom as late and foreign in Israel has been the quite proper recognition that the compilation of our biblical wisdom books was postexilic. Yet archeology has made it increasingly clear that wisdom was already ancient by the time Israel became a self-conscious community; and the biblical parallels to this ancient material lead to the conclusion that much of it had circulated in Hebrew widom circles for many years before the final editing of the canonical examples. Albright says that "Proverbs teems with Canaanitisms",[5] and would place the content of the entire work in the pre-exilic period.[6] H.L. Ginsberg has identified *hokmōth*, the name of Wisdom in Prov. 9 and elsewhere, as a Phoenician term.[7] The connection of Hebrew wisdom with Egyptian thought has long been recognized, and the literary connection of Prov. 22:17-23:14 with the *Instruction of Amenemopet* has been widely accepted for some time. The recent work of Edmund Gordon, as we have seen, shows the dominant forms of biblical proverbs to have *written* precedents early in the second millenium B.C..

That the custodians of wisdom shared with the priests and prophets in the intellectual and spiritual leadership of Israel has generally been assumed. And the frequently cited words of Jer. 18:18 bear out the point. But while the priests and the prophets can be seen, despite the

---

4   James Barr, *The Semantics of Biblical Language* (London: Oxford University Press, 1961), especially pp. 8-88.
5   Albright, "Some Canaanite-Phoenician . . .", p. 9.
6   *Op. cit.*, p. 13.
7   *Op cit.*, p. 8.

anti-cultic fulminations of an Amos or a Jeremiah, to have had much in common,[8] the wise men frequently seem to stand alone. "But", as R.B.Y. Scott has intimated, "the wisdom teachers may have played a larger role even in the earlier period than is suggested by the surviving literature and the present structure of the Hebrew Bible."[9]

To be sure, the wise man sometimes seems to be denounced by the prophet, and generally he stands aloof from both cultic concerns and the critical events of Israel's history. But several things need to be said in his defense.

First of all, we do not see the wise man at any point standing deliberately against the cult or the sacred history. As von Rad has pointed out, these matters were simply not his primary concern. [10] He was much more interested in helping man to live out his life to its fullest potentiality, and devoted himself to pointing the way.[11]

Secondly, we find in Proverbs not infrequent mention of the importance of religion in the good life. [12] For the wise man the fear of the Lord was the beginning of wisdom. It was not, however, the end; that was rather the understanding of human affairs and the way to a full and happy life. And it does not seem to be any more legitimate to place the sage outside the mainstream of Hebrew life and thought because of his more 'secular' calling than to jump to the conclusion that a modern social worker or marriage counselor is, by virtue of his vocation, un-Christian or un-Jewish or un-American.

In the third place, those passages which may be cited to illustrate the prophet's antipathy to the Hebrew wise man do not really do so. If, for example, we check the passages noted by Scott in his article, "Priesthood, Prophecy, Wisdom, and the Knowledge of God", to

---

8   R.B.Y. Scott, "Priesthood, Prophecy, Wisdom and the Knowledge of God", *Journal of Biblical Literature*, Vol LXXX (March, 1961), pp. 8-9.

9   *Op. cit.*, p. 4.

10   von Rad, *Old Testament Theology*, p. 435.

11   See Fleming James, "Some Aspects of the Religion of Proverbs", *Journal of Biblical Literature*, Vol. LI, Part 1 (1932), pp. 31-39.

12   Prov. 1:7, 29; 2:5; 3:7; 8:13; 9:10; 10:27; 14:27; 15:16, 33; 16:6; 19:23; 22:4; 23:17; 24:21. In both Egyptian and Babylonian wisdom there seems to be this same regard for religion. The beliefs reflected, of course, are quite different, but one gets the impression that the wise man generally accepted his religious heritage without question. And the practice of religion was seen as essential to the prosperous and happy life.

show that "Isaiah and Jeremiah scorn the wise men of their time", [13] what do we find?

In two passages we find that arrogance and pride stand condemned:

> Woe to those who are wise in their own eyes,
>   and shrewd in their own sight.[14]

> Thus says the LORD: "Let not the wise man glory in his wisdom, let not the mighty man glory in his might, let not the rich man glory in his riches; but let him who glories glory in this, that he understands and knows me, that I am the LORD . . . "[15]

One passage singles out for rebuke certain *Egyptian* wise men in an oracle against Egypt:

> The princes of Zoan are utterly foolish;
>   the wise counselors of Pharaoh give stupid counsel.
> How can you say to Pharaoh,
>   "I am a son of the wise,
>   a son of ancient kings"?
> Where then are your wise men?
>   Let them tell you and make known
>   what the LORD of hosts has purposed against Egypt.[16]

Another passage threatens the end of wisdom in the land as *punishment*, thus pointing indirectly to its value:

> therefore, behold, I will again
>   do marvelous things with this people,
>   wonderful and marvelous;
> and the wisdom of their wise men shall perish
>   and the discernment of their discerning men shall be hid.[17]

---

13 Scott, "Priesthood . . .", p. 4.
14 Isa. 5:21. Johannes Lindblom, "Wisdom in the Old Testament Prophets", *Wisdom in Israel and the Ancient Near East*, eds. H.H.Rowley, Martin Noth, D. Winton Thomas (= Supplements to *Vetus Testamentum*, Vol. III) (Leiden: E.J. Brill, 1960), p. 194; Ranston, *op. cit.*, p. 20.
15 Jer. 9:23-24; Lindblom, *op. cit.*, p. 195; Ranston, *loc. cit*.
16 Isa. 19:11-12.
17 Isa. 29:14; Ranston, *loc. cit.*

If the prophet really stood unalterably opposed to the wisdom tradition he would surely see its impending confusion more as a blessing than as punishment. And in the final passage noted by Scott we see only a reference to the limitations of human understanding, and it is doubtful whether the professional wise man is intended: "Who is the man so wise that he can understand this? To whom has the mouth of the LORD spoken, that he may declare it?"[18] Far from opposing the wise man, this passage echoes him. One need only recall the whirlwind speech in Job or cite this passage from Proverbs:

> Be not wise in your own eyes;
>   fear the LORD, and turn away from evil.[19]

In no case, then, do these passages indicate the antagonism they are supposed to show. But the following excerpt might also be cited:

> How can you say, "We are wise,
>   and the law of the LORD is with us"?
> But, behold, the false pen of the scribes
>   has made it into a lie.
> The wise men shall be put to shame,
>   they shall be dismayed and taken;
> lo, they have rejected the word of the LORD,
>   and what wisdom is in them? [20]

Yet one need not see these words as directed against the wise as a class any more than we might take the words against false prophecy as a condemnation of prophecy in general. In fact we read in the very next verse that "from prophet to priest every one deals falsely". And we see in Jer. 18:18 that this prophet apparently saw the departure of wisdom as being a calamity of the same order as the perishing of law from the priest and the word from the prophet!

Not only does the prophet not stand in opposition to the wise man, but he values wisdom so highly that he denounces its false practitioners — as he also denounces false prophets — and forecasts the loss of

---

18   Jer. 9:12; Ranston, *loc. cit.*
19   Prov. 3:7. These passages are, to be sure, from later material. But see the Babylonian and Egyptian verses quoted below, p. 121.
20   Jer. 8:8-9.

wisdom as a part of God's terrible judgment. Wisdom, in fact, is
sometimes seen as an attribute of God.[21]

In the fourth place there is considerable evidence to show that the
prophet and priest stood in the wise man's debt. And it is the proverb
which frequently helps us to establish this indebtedness. We turn now
to an investigation of wisdom's influence upon the prophetic and
priestly traditions.

THE PROPHETIC TRADITION

While it has been customary in the past to talk about the influence of
the prophets on the wisdom tradition, it now seems more correct to
see the influence moving in the opposite direction. The idea, of
course, is not new. It has been suggested in various ways by Lindblom,
Rankin, Gressmann, Fichtner, and Jacob, [22] but has been a long time
taking hold.

While we would not want to insist that the prophets exerted no
influence at all upon the wise men, particularly those of postexilic
Judaism, one may at the same time contend that wisdom constituted
a major influence upon the canonical prophets. The argument for this
is relatively simple: It is frequently much easier to assume, where
parallels are to be seen in the two traditions, that the prophets were
influenced by a centuries-old wisdom tradition than it is to account
for similarities by postulating an influence upon wisdom from a movement which found its proper voice in Israel only in the years following
upon the establishment of the monarchy. Where Yahwism is reflected
in wisdom, of course, there may be prophetic influence; but it is more
likely to stem from the Israelite Faith which preceded the rise of the
great prophets. The argument is further strengthened when one can

---

21   Isa. 10:13; 11:2; 28:29; Jer. 10:12; 51:15; See William McKane's *Prophets
and Wise Men* for a contrary argument. It seems less than convincing to us
because of its overheavy reliance upon vocabulary study, its lack of sufficient
attention to non-Israelite wisdom sources and its use of prophets' words against
particular wise men (some of them Egyptian) to demonstrate the prophets'
antipathy for the wise as a class. William McKane, *Prophets and Wise Men*
(= *Studies in Biblical Theology*, No. 44) (London: SCM Press Ltd., 1965).
22   John F. Priest, "Where is Wisdom to be Placed?" *The Journal of Bible and
Religion*, Vol. XXXI (October, 1963), p. 279.

cite in the prophets rather striking parallels in form and content to the earlier wisdom traditions of Egypt, Sumer and Canaan.

The dominant influence appears to come through the use of the proverb, both in its popular undeveloped form and in its more artistic shape. Although many of these proverbs may have circulated among the people, others surely were known in learned circles, particularly those displaying parallel form. Here are a few examples:

> The ox knows its owner,
>   and the ass its master's crib;
> . . . . [23]

> Your silver has become dross,
>   your wine mixed with water.[24]

> Shall the axe vaunt itself over him who hews with it?
>   or the saw magnify itself against him who wields it? [25]

> Does he who plows for sowing plow continually?
>   Does he continually open and' harrow the ground? [26]

> Dill is not threshed with a threshing sledge,
>   nor is a cart wheel rolled over cummin;
> . . . . [27]

> Can the prey be taken from the mighty,
>   or the captives of a tyrant be rescued? [28]

> Can the Ethiopian change his skin
>   or the leopard his spots? [29]

> Like the partridge that gathers a brood which she did not hatch,
>   so is he who gets riches but not by right;
> in the midst of his days they will leave him,
>   and at his end he will be a fool.[30]

23   Isa. 1:3.
24   Isa. 1:22.
25   Isa. 10:15.
26   Isa. 28:24.
27   Isa. 28:27.
28   Isa. 49:24.
29   Jer. 13:23.
30   Jer. 17:11.

What has straw in common with wheat? [31]

The time is not near to build houses; this city is the cauldron, and we are the flesh.[32]

Like mother, like daughter.[33]

For they sow the wind,
 and they shall reap the whirlwind.[34]

Do two walk together,
 unless they have made an appointment?
Does a lion roar in the forest,
 when he has no prey?
Does a young lion cry out from its den,
 if he has taken nothing?
Does a bird fall in a snare on the earth,
 when there is no trap for it?
Does a snare spring up from the ground
 when it has taken nothing?
Is a trumpet blown in the city,
 and the people are not afraid? [35]

Do horses run upon rocks?
 Does one plow the sea with oxen? [36]

For the stone will cry out from the wall,
 and the beam from the woodwork respond.[37]

These and other examples [38] would seem to indicate clearly the influence of proverbs. Even when they may be the prophet's own creation, their form, we believe, betrays familiarity with the maxims of the wise. If the parallel form in general derives from the proverb, [39] then

---

31 Jer. 23:28.
32 Ezek. 11:3.
33 Ezek. 16:44.
34 Hos. 8:7.
35 Amos 3:3-6.
36 Amos 6:12. R.S.V. translation according to the emendation בַּבָּקָר יָם against the MT בַּבְּקָרִים.
37 Hab. 2:11.
38 Isa. 3:10-11; 32:5-8; 33:11; 65:8; Jer. 8:4; 13:12; 15:12; 31:29; Ezek. 12:22; Hos. 7:4; 10:1,12-13; Amos 3:8; 5:19.
39 Above, pp. 92-93.

of course one may see this influence throughout much more of the oracular material. Our evidence is admittedly slim, but the possibility is real.

In addition to these examples of proverb usage, one has in Amos 1:3,6,9,11,13; 2:1,4,6 the use of a numerical device common in wisdom literature, especially Prov. 30.[40] We have already noted a Canaanite example of such usage[41] and its use in the *Words of Ahiqar*.[42] Thus the phrase, "For three transgressions of Damascus, and for four . . ." from Amos [43] echoes the "Three things are never satisfied; four never say 'enough': . . ." from Proverbs.[44] Terrien points out several similar numerical formulae in Job 33:14; 40:5; Ps. 62:11, and in the Ugaritic poem of *Keret*.[45]

An interesting parallel of similes can be found in Jer. 17:5-8, Ps. 1 and in a passage from Amenemopet.[46] Lindblom cites the following further examples of wisdom's influence upon the prophets: Nathan's parable, Isaiah's allegory of the vineyard, the parable of the farmer in Isa. 28, Ezekiel's many allegories, various similes, the rhetorical question, the dialogue between man and God (as in Amos 7:7f.; 8:2; Jer. 1:11f., 13; 24:3), the 'reiteration and concatenation of ideas and phrases' (Hos. 11:23f.; Isa. 65:13-14; Jer. 15:2f.; 51:20-23; Amos 3:3-60), and the use of the term *mûsār* in Jeremiah.[47]

---

40 Samuel Terrien, "Amos and Wisdom", *Israel's Prophetic Heritage*, eds. Bernard W. Anderson, Walter Harrelson (New York: Harper & Brothers, 1962), pp. 109-10. Hans Walter Wolff finds Amos' "spiritual homeland" among the wise men of the Israelite clans, and uses this postulated background to explain the reflections of wisdom in Amos. Hans Walter Wolff, *Amos' Geistige Heimat* (= *Wissenschaftliche Monographien zum Alten und Neuen Testament*, Vol. XVIII) (Neukirchen-Vluyn: Neukirchener Verlag, 1964). Our conclusions obviously point more in the direction of court schools as the primary point of influence. A work that is more compatible with ours here is Hermisson, *op. cit.*, especially pp. 113-29.

41 Above, p. 55.

42 Above, p. 49.

43 Amos 1:3.

44 Prov. 30:15.

45 Terrien, *op. cit.*, pp. 109-10.

46 James Henry Breasted, *Development of Religion and Thought in Ancient Egypt* (New York: Charles Scribner's Sons, 1912), pp. 364-65; E.A. Wallis Budge, *The Teaching of Amenem-apt, Son of Kanekht* (London: M. Hopkinson & Co., 1924), p. 107. Pritchard, *Texts*, p. 422.

47 Lindblom, *op. cit.*, pp. 201-04.

Terrien finds the following reflections of sapiential material in Amos, besides those we have already seen: the use of the word *sôd*, the use of the word *nekōḥâ*, the use of the term *wayyitrōp* with the noun *ap*, reference to the nation as 'Isaac'.[48]

If one compares the content of Proverbs with that of the prophetic literature one observes a great similarity with regard to ethics. This, of course, needs no argument. It has been observed for a very long time, although it used to be stated that the wise men popularized and made individual application of the prophetic teaching. Ranston, for example, wrote that "the Sages took over these messages [of the prophets], individualized them and expressed their essential truths in a happier and less irritating fashion".[49]

Now, we believe, one must see the ethics of the sage as providing a part of the foundation upon which the prophet stood. To be sure, the prophet brought to his task the earnest fervor of his nature, his greater concern for the nation than for the individual, his sense of Yahweh's intimate involvement in current history and in his own life. But as to what constituted ethical behavior, he offered little that was new. As Porteous has put it,

What specially distinguished the prophets was not the fundamental novelty of what they had to say about God's requirements, though there were times when it was given to them to say something new, but the fact that there were times when inherited truth and the reflections to which it had given rise became fused into a compelling conviction and a sense of obligation to surrender heart and will completely to the command of God. In the brilliant light of this personal relationship truth became existential and compelled to action . . .[50]

If we look beyond our biblical wisdom books we find the same high ethical ideals not only in Egypt but in ancient Sumer as well: condemnation of the use of false weights and measures, care of the widow,

---

48   Terrien, *op. cit.*, pp. 112-13. For a critique of Terrien's conclusions see Crenshaw, "The Influence of the Wise upon Amos", pp. 44-46.
49   Ranston, *op. cit.*, p. 19.
50   Norman W. Porteous, "The Basis of the Ethical Teaching of the Prophets", *Studies in Old Testament Prophecy*, ed. H.H, Rowley (Edinburgh: T. & T. Clark, 1946), p. 152.

avoidance of bad company, the dangers of association with immoral women, the virtues of honesty, fidelity, industry, love of family, humility, circumspect speech – all are there. Kramer writes,

... on the level of ethics and morals, the documents reveal that the Sumerians cherished and valued goodness and truth, law and order, justice and freedom, wisdom and learning, courage and loyalty – in short, all of man's most desirable virtues and qualities. Even mercy and compassion were treasured and practiced, at least in the breach, to judge from the numerous references to the special protective treatment accorded to widows, orphans, and refugees as well as to the poor and oppressed.[51]

It is interesting to observe here that half a century ago Causse took exception to a statement of Amélineau which, while premature then, was prophetic of things to come. Amélineau stated that

... longtemps avant Moïse, longtemps avant les prophètes, longtemps avant les philosophes grecs l'Egypt avait su trouver des maximes qui peuvent supporter la comparison avec les préceptes les plus élevés des Prophètes hébreux, des philosophes grecs et du Christ.[52]

Furthermore, there is in the extra-biblical wisdom a firm belief in the doctrine of rewards and punishments. As we read in one of the Sumerian-Akkadian tablets,

Commit no crime, and fear [of your god] will not consume you.
Slander no one, and then grief [will not] reach your heart.[53]

With continuing archeological research in the Near East we become increasingly convinced of the truth of Rankin's words, written over thirty years ago:

When we view Hebrew humanism as being a native product of the Wisdom literature which has its roots deep in that Oriental wisdom which is much older than the earliest writing prophets of Israel, we

---

51   Kramer, *The Sumerians . . .*, p. 264.
52   A. Causse, "Introduction à l'étude de la sagesse juive", *Revue d'Histoire et de Philosophie religieuses*, Vol. I (1921), p. 58.
53   Lambert, *op. cit.*, p. 247.

may more justly conclude that the prophetic teaching on its social
side was inspired and nurtured by Israel's wisdom writers, who as
composers of maxims and ethical instructors were active from the
time of the establishment of the state under Solomon.[54]

Three other similarities of content can also be noted: the theodicies
of Jer. 12:1-13 and Habakkuk 1-2 and that of the 'Sumerian Job';[55] the
priority of righteousness over ritual seen in Amos and Jeremiah and
Prov. 21:3; 21:27; 28:9, and anticipated in the *Instruction for King
Merikare*: "More acceptable is the character of one upright of heart
than the ox of the evildoer",[56] and the universality of Amos' ethic, so
common in the wisdom literature.[57]

Both in matters of form and content, then, Israel's prophets are
indebted to the wise man. But we may push the case one step further.
It is generally acknowledged that before the establishment of the
Israelite monarchy the Hebrew prophets were bound together in
bands, given to remarkable ecstatic behavior, almost devoid of ethical
concern, politically uninvolved except when hired to bring about poli-
tical good fortune. After the rise of the monarchy, however, there was
a dramatic change in the prophet: he became a champion of high
ethics, as were the wise men; he became more involved politically, as
the sages had been for many centuries; he was less ecstatic, more like
the wise man; he spoke from his own experience rather than in con-
cert with a prophetic band, as frequently did the wise man; he used
many of the forms of address familiar in wisdom writings, proverbs in
particular; he is sometimes associated with those who can write (and
so his words may be preserved as were Jeremiah's by Baruch), as were
the sages. Amos reflects a universal ethic, as did the wise men; Jeremiah and Ezekiel reflect individualism, long characteristic of wisdom;
Jeremiah and Habakkuk contain theodicies, seen in wisdom as far
back as Sumerian times. Can it be mere coincidence that this drastic

---

[54]   O.S. Rankin, *Israel's Wisdom Literature* (Edinburgh: T. & T. Clark, 1936),
p. 14.
[55]   Samuel Noah Kramer, " 'Man and his God': A Sumerian Variation on the
'Job' Motif", *Wisdom in Israel and in the Ancient Near East*, eds. H.H. Rowley,
Martin Noth, D. Winton Thomas (= Supplements to *Vetus Testamentum*, Vol.
III) (Leiden: E.J. Brill, 1960), pp. 170-82.
[56]   Pritchard, *Texts*, p. 417.
[57]   Amos 9:7.

change took place at about the same time that the scribe-wise man began to play an important role in the leadership of the nation? Such coincidence does not seem likely. It is much more reasonable to assume that the prophets, for all their uniqueness, stood solidly upon the shoulders of the wise. It is interesting to observe that Eichrodt notes a quite similar change as he describes the transition from the pre-monarchic נביאים to the classical prophets, but ignores the possibility of any wisdom influence in the process. He sees the uniqueness of these late prophetic voices as stemming in part from the old נביאים , but deriving primarily from the intensely personal encounter between prophet and Yahweh. While we should not deny the pre-eminence of this personal element, we yet must see the wisdom influence as playing a rather considerable role. It is difficult to understand how, as Eichrodt believes, the נביאים could 'degenerate' as a result of their position in royal circles, while at the same time the classical prophets could become almost entirely liberated from this same general background. It seems to us that Eichrodt sets the stage beautifully for explaining wisdom's contact with the prophetic tradition and influence upon it, only then to ignore it completely.[58] Actually, it has been suggested that Isaiah was himself a court scribe, at least during a part of his career. He did, after all, have access to the king; he seems to have composed court annals;[59] his familiarity with diplomatic matters could help explain his consuming interest in them.[60] Robert Anderson has even suggested that Isaiah was a court counselor to Uzziah, a prophet during the time of Ahaz, and a counselor again under Hezekiah.[61] As a scribe he will have had 'disciples' to teach or, as the Hebrew puts it, "the ones taught"[62] or the "children".[63] However this may be, we can little doubt that Isaiah

---

58 See Walther Eichrodt, *Theology of the Old Testament*, trans. J.A. Baker, Vol. I (*The Old Testament Library*) (Philadelphia: The Westminster Press, 1961), pp. 309-91.
59 II Chron. 26:22.
60 Robert T. Anderson, "Was Isaiah a Scribe? ", *Journal of Biblical Literature*, Vol. LXXIX (March, 1960), pp. 57-58.
61 *Op. cit.*, p. 58.
62 Isa. 8:16. Anderson, *loc. cit.*
63 Isa. 8:18. Anderson, *loc. cit.*

was at least in a position to be greatly influenced by the wise man; and it is our opinion that he was.[64]

What we see in the prophets, then, is an explosive fusion of ancient wisdom, the sacred traditions of Israel's history and the compelling force of the prophetic personality speaking out of deep religious experience and sensitivity to Yahweh's immediate demand.

THE PRIESTLY TRADITION

As we turn to the question of the possible influence of wisdom upon the priestly traditions we note that in both ancient Sumer, later Babylonian culture and in Egypt there was a close relationship between priests and wise men, this relationship being frequently seen in the proximity of schools and temples. [65] In the absence of evidence to the contrary we may expect that this close relationship also obtained in Israel. As Mowinckel has written,

There is every reason to believe that the school for scribes in Jerusalem [which he would have founded by Solomon], as elsewhere in the Orient, was closely connected with the Temple; this is apparent by the very fact that the 'wisdom literature' of Israel was reckoned among the canonical writings.

Scholars have often distinguished too sharply between the different 'classes' of the 'intelligentsia' in ancient Israel: priests, prophets, scribes, wise men, etc., as if they were sharply defined social and functional 'classes'.[66]

---

64   It was Johannes Fichtner who seems first to have suggested that Isaiah was influenced by the wisdom tradition; in fact he argued that Isaiah had at one time been a member of the community of the wise. Johannes Fichtner, "Jesaja unter den Weisen", *Theologische Literaturzeitung*, LXXIV (February, 1949), columns 75-80. A recent study that reinforces Fichtner's principal argument, while discounting the possibility of Isaiah's ever having been a wise man, is James William Whedbee's *Isaiah and Wisdom*, Ph. D. Dissertation (Ann Arbor: University Microfilms, Inc., 1969).

65   Salo W. Baron, *A Social and Religious History of the Jews*, Vol. I (New York: Columbia University Press, 1952), pp. 150-51; Burrows, *op. cit.*, p. 183; Erman, *op. cit.*, p. 185; Rylaarsdam, *Revelation . . .*, pp. 11-13.

66   Sigmund Mowinckel, *The Psalms in Israel's Worship*, Vol. II, trans. D.R. Ap-Thomas (New York: Abingdon Press, 1962), p. 104.

At this point we shall look at two features of the priestly tradition which appear to show the most obvious influences of the wise men: psalms and law.

Psalms

The most obvious reflections of wisdom in the Psalms are of course to be found in the so-called 'wisdom psalms': Ps. 1; 19:7-14; 32:8-11; 34:12-23; 37; 49; 73; 94:8-23; 111; 112; 119; 127; 128. [67] Here not only the content but the form reflects the proverb, even as it was known in ancient Egypt and Sumer. [68] In addition to these examples Mowinckel would see the "testimonies of the psalms of thanksgiving and their exhortations to the congregation" as displaying the content of wisdom and the form of the proverb. [69]

But furthermore, we may suspect a more pervasive influence in the parallelism of the Psalter in general. This suggestion is admittedly quite speculative, but at the same time it is worth remembering that our most ancient examples of parallelism come out of learned scribal circles and that we do have examples of parallelism resulting from the proverb riddle. [70]

Although Mowinckel sees a mutual influence taking place between the psalmists and the wise men, [71] and while Engnell would have the wisdom literature deriving from the cult, [72] we are inclined to see the influence rather more on the side of wisdom. There are three reasons why one may see it so: (1) Not only is the proverb form exceedingly ancient, but it pervades the cultures of many primitive peoples where nothing like the developed cultic life of Israel is to be found; furthermore, Herskovits says of the African Dahomeans that "the song of

---

67   Gemser, *op. cit.*, p. 3. It is difficult, of course, to be precise in the classification of wisdom psalms. Some helpful guidelines are set forth in Roland E. Murphy's "A Consideration of the Classification 'Wisdom Psalms' ", *Congress Volume, Bonn, 1962,* ed. P.A.H. de Boer (= Supplements to *Vetus Testamentum*, Vol. IX) (Leiden: E.J. Brill, 1963), pp. 156-67.

68   Gressmann, *op. cit.,* pp. 30-31.

69   Mowinckel, *op. cit.*, pp. 105-06.

70   Above, pp. 92-93. Note also the numerical formula of Ps. 62:11.

71   Mowinckel, *op. cit*., p. 105.

72   Bentzen, *op. cit.*, Vol. I, p. 174.

praise to the gods, and to the living and the dead, draws on the common store of proverbs for theme, imagery, and moral". [73] (2) The genesis of the parallel form, as we have indicated, may lie in the proverb-riddle. And (3) we can see the probable influence of wisdom on Babylonian hymns. Lambert tells us that ethical injunctions "are a well-known feature of some Sumerian hymns", [74] and Böhl believes that part of the *Shamash Hymn* was borrowed from wisdom material. [75] If Böhl is correct, then we have an ancient precedent of wisdom influencing the cult rather than the reverse.

Law

We have already noted the close connection which is frequently found between proverbs and law, and we have seen some evidence of this connection in the culture of ancient Israel. We have also seen in the proverbs of Babylonia, Egypt and Israel what we could call a moral imperative form. Not that this form is always cast in what grammarians would call the imperative mood, but it is put in the form of a second singular moral injunction or prohibition. This form, particularly the prohibition, is frequently found in the Egyptian literature and seems to be reflected in the book of Proverbs as well. [76]

It is here suggested that this form, particularly as it is found in the proverb material of Egypt, quite possibly lies behind the apodictic law of Israel; and we cite the following comparisons as evidence of a possible relationship, noting interesting parallels in content as well as form:

> Honor your father and your mother, that your days may be long in the land which the LORD your God gives you. [77]

---

73   Melville J. and Frances S. Herskovits, *Dahomean Narrative: A Cross-Cultural Analysis* (=*Northwestern University African Studies*, No. 1) (Evanston: Northwestern University Press, 1958), p. 57.
74   Lambert, *op. cit.*, p. 118.
75   *Op. cit.* p. 123.
76   Humbert, *op. cit.*, pp. 64, 66; Above, pp. 62-63. For very helpful and more detailed studies of these prohibitions see Gerstenberger, *op. cit.*, and Richter, *op. cit.* These scholars find the principal origins of Israel's apodictic law in old Hebrew wisdom.
77   Exod. 20:12.

Double the food which thou givest to thy mother, and carry her as she carried (thee) . . .[78]

* * *

You shall not kill.[79]

Do not slaughter: it is not of advantage to thee.[80]

* * *

You shall not commit adultery.[81]

. . . Be on thy guard against a woman from abroad, who is not known in her (own) town. Do not stare at her when she passes by. Do not know her carnally: a deep water, whose windings one knows not, a woman who is far away from her husband . . .[82]

* * *

You shall not steal.[83]

Guard thyself against robbing the oppressed
And against overbearing the disabled.[84]

* * *

You shall not bear false witness against your neighbor.[85]

Do not bear witness with false words,
Nor support another person (thus) with thy tongue.[86]

* * *

You shall not covet your neighbor's house; you shall not covet your neighbor's wife, or his manservant, or his maidservant, or his ox, or his ass, or anything that is your neighbor's.[87]

[78]   *Instruction of Ani*, Pritchard, *Texts*, p. 420.
[79]   Exod. 20:13.
[80]   *Instruction for King Merikare*, Pritchard, *Texts*, p. 415.
[81]   Exod. 20:14.
[82]   *Instruction of Ani*, Pritchard, *Texts*, p. 420.
[83]   Exod. 20:15.
[84]   *Instruction of Amenemopet*, Pritchard, *Texts*, p. 422.
[85]   Exod. 20:16.
[86]   *Instruction of Amenemopet*, Pritchard, *Texts*, p. 423.
[87]   Exod. 20:17.

Do not be covetous at a division. Do not be greedy, unless (it be) for thy (own) portion. Do not be covetous against thy own kindred.[88]

Be not greedy for the property of a poor man,
Nor hunger for his bread.[89]

* * *

You shall not afflict any widow or orphan.[90]

... do not oppress the widow ...[91]

Do not recognize a widow if thou catchest her in the fields,
Nor fail to be indulgent to her reply.[92]

* * *

You shall not delay to offer him the fullness of your harvest and from the outflow of your presses.[93]

Make the offering table flourish, increase the loaves, and add to the daily offerings. It is an advantage to him who does it.[94]

* * *

You shall not pervert the justice due to your poor in his suit.[95]

Do not distinguish the son of a man from a poor man, (but) take to thyself a man because of the work of his hands.[96]

Do not confuse a man in the law court,
Nor *divert* the righteous man.
Give not thy attention (only) to him clothed in white,
Nor give consideration to him that is unkempt.[97]

* * *

---

88   *Instruction of the Vizier Ptahhotep*, Pritchard, *Texts*, p. 413.
89   *Instruction of Amenemopet*, Pritchard, *Texts*, p. 423.
90   Exod. 22:22.
91   *Instruction for King Merikare*, Pritchard, *Texts*, p. 415.
92   *Instruction of Amenemopet*, Pritchard, *Texts*, p. 424.
93   Exod. 22:29.
94   *Instruction for King Merikare*, Pritchard, *Texts*, p. 416.
95   Exod. 23:6.
96   *Instruction for King Merikare*, Pritchard, *Texts*, p. 415.
97   *Instruction of Amenemopet*, Pritchard, *Texts*, p. 424.

And you shall take no bribe, for a bribe blinds the officials, and subverts the cause of those who are in the right.[98]

Do not accept the bribe of a powerful man,
Nor oppress for him the disabled.[99]

As striking as these parallels are, they become even more so when one considers that four purport to come from the contending ruler of Egypt for his son Merikare, and one from the Vizier Ptahhotep. That is, they take on the appearance of royal decrees. And although they are ostensibly written for the sons of the authors, their subsequent preservation and circulation testify to their wider application. The introductory and concluding words of the authors, whether authentic or provided by later generations, also indicate that they were probably revered almost as divine oracles. From the concluding lines of the *Instruction for King Merikare* we have this passage:

> Thou shouldst do nothing harmful *with regard to me, who have given* all the laws concerning the king . . . Behold I have spoken to thee the profitable matters of my (very) belly. Mayest thou act on what is established before thy face.[100]

And from the introductory words of the *Instruction of the Vizier Ptahhotep* we read,

> The beginning of the expression of good speech, spoken by the Hereditary Prince and Count, God's Father and God's Beloved, eldest son of the king, of his body, the Mayor and Vizier, Ptahhotep . . .[101]

The fact that these two collections are related to the royal house of Egypt give them no little authority, for

the king of Egypt was a god . . . This was not stated in a nice compact formulation which made the pharaoh the personification of the land

---

98   Exod. 23:8.
99   *Instruction of Amenemopet*, Pritchard, *Texts*, p. 424.
100   *Instruction for King Merikare*, Pritchard, *Texts*, pp. 417-18.
101   *Instruction of the Vizier Ptahhotep*, Pritchard, *Texts*, p. 412. See also *The Divine Attributes of Pharaoh*, Pritchard, *Texts*, p. 431.

of Egypt or even embodied rule as a personified principle. But the supreme god, Rē, entrusted the land to his son, the king. From the Old Kingdom on, an effective title for the Egyptian pharaoh was the 'Son of Rē'.[102]

As one king's minister is reported to have said, "Now his majesty knows what takes place. There is nothing at all which he does not know. He is (the god of wisdom) Thoth in everything: there is no subject which he has not comprehended." [103]

As for similar injunctions penned by lesser lights, they could conceivably be quotations which were at one time regarded as divine decrees. The fact that they were preserved and valued alongside the words of kings would tend to suggest that their authority was not far less. And the words of some scribes, we may imagine, were almost as highly revered. Imhotep, after all, was deified by later generations. [104] Furthermore, it is significant that the instructions which are not attributed to the pharaoh, or to a member of the royal family, are sometimes taken to be the words of state officials. For, as Frankfort has written, "they stand apart as a class — the Royal Kinsmen. In other words, those to whom power has been delegated shared in some degree the mysterious essence which differentiated the king from all men."[105]

We may hazard the following conclusion at any rate: The form of the moral imperative or 'apodictic law' found in the Exodus Decalogue, the Covenant Code, and repeated elsewhere in the Old Testament, is not unique with Israel, but is also to be seen in the wisdom

---

102   John A. Wilson, "Egypt: The Nature of the Universe", *The Intellectual Adventure of Ancient Man*, eds. H. Frankfort, *et al.* (Chicago: University of Chicago Press, 1946), p. 71.

103   Wilson, *op. cit.*, p. 76. In the absence of any known legal code from ancient Egypt, some scholars would see the words of the reigning kings as constituting actual law, thus making impossible the coexistence of any written statements. See F. Charles Fensham, "Widow, Orphan, and the Poor in Ancient Near Eastern Legal and Wisdom Literature," *Journal of Near Eastern Studies,* Vol. XXI (Jan.-Oct., 1962), p. 132; John A. Wilson, *The Culture of Ancient Egypt* ("Phoenix Books") (Chicago: The University of Chicago Press, 1951), pp. 49-50.

104   Above, pp. 37-38.

105   Henri Frankfort, *Kingship and the Gods* (Chicago: The University of Chicago Press, 1948), p. 52.

literature of Egypt. Furthermore, there is a striking similarity in the content of some of these imperatives to those of the Old Testament. And finally, there is a good reason to suspect that at least some, if not all, of the Egyptian injunctions were understood to be of divine or semi-divine origin, as were those in the legal material of Israel.

It may be objected here that whereas advice or counsel leaves the matter of application to the hearer (and so contradictory injunctions may easily co-exist), apodictic command enjoins absolute obedience. Consequently it may seem questionable to relate counsel so closely to law. Yet it should be observed that the apodictic command, so general as it often was, left considerable freedom for interpretation and application. As a recent writer has said of the laws of the Covenant Code, "The scarcity of commentary may indicate that they were chiefly guidelines or precepts which elders, priests and judges used to decide how to treat a case."[106] Also, one may expect that as counsel, especially divine counsel, became increasingly revered over the centuries, it also became correspondingly less subject to qualification.[107]

One cannot, of course, establish any literary dependence on the basis of such evidence. But that there is a direct connection between these Egyptian injunctions and those of the Old Testament would appear most likely. If, as we have argued, the rise of the Israelite monarchy under Solomon and his successors saw a great increase in the number of scribes; and if, as is most probable, there was continuing influence from Egypt at this time, then the presence of the imperative form in the E material would not be at all unnatural.

Another possibility, certainly, is that Moses himself was acquainted with this type of material, and so reflected it in the composition of the Decalogue. If we accept the biblical tradition of his relationship to Pharaoh's court, and if he was educated there, he could hardly *not* have been familiar with this form of instruction.

---

106   H. Keith Beebe, *The Old Testament, An Introduction to Its Literary, Historical, and Religious Traditions* (Belmont, California: Dickenson Publishing Company, Inc., 1970), p. 100.

107   If Schmid's interpretation is correct, we can trace the 'dogmatization' of wisdom not only in Israel, but in Egypt and Mesopotamia as well. See Hans Heinrich Schmid, *Wesen und Geschichte der Weisheit: Eine Untersuchung zur Altorientalischen und Israelitischen Weisheitsliteratur* (Berlin: Verlag Alfred Töpelmann, 1966).

It is generally agreed that the 'case law' of Israel was related to the legal traditions of surrounding cultures. Now, if we are correct in our present argument, we must see the apodictic form as similarly related. The priest, like the prophet, stood in the wise man's debt; and the most sacred ordinances of the covenant community owed their form, if not their content as well, to the lowly proverb.

5. SKEPTICISM AND HEBREW RELIGION

We have thus far been confining our attention primarily to matters of function and form. But now it becomes necessary to discuss content. For if, as we have maintained, the contribution of Israel was negligible so far as the form or function of proverbs is concerned, may she not have added significant content?

Here too we are hard pressed to find uniqueness. To be sure, almost all vestiges of polytheism have disappeared; and the God Yahweh has come to play an important role. But whether the wise man's attitude toward Yahweh is fundamentally different from that of his foreign colleagues toward their divinities is a moot question. There is a more democratic spirit in the proverbs of Israel, however; and this may be reflective of the Covenant Faith. Also peculiarly Israelite may be the stronger emphasis upon morality and justice, as opposed to the ritual concerns of some Babylonian writing. And naturally there is no reflection on any belief in an afterlife such as we find in ancient Egypt.

But still, we look in vain for references to Israel as the people of God or to the sacred history of the elect nation. The cult is of small concern, and reference to priests or prophets is not to be found.

It may well be that the proverbs of Israel took on added meaning as they came to be associated with the Yahwistic tradition. We may well imagine that the oppression of the poor, adultery, bribery and covetousness inveighed against by the sages came to be seen as breaches of covenant, as violations of the fundamental relationship between Israelite man and Yahweh.[1] Particularly as proverbs were taken into the priestly and prophetic traditions would this seem to be the case. But whether the sages themselves so understood their unique heritage, particularly in pre-exilic and exilic times — this is not so clear. It is

1   von Rad, *Old Testament Theology*, p. 437.

true, of course, that Isreal's wisdom which followed upon the exile
became increasingly a part of the religion of Yahweh. By the time the
sage of Israel could claim that the fear of Yahweh was the beginning
of wisdom,[2] we may rightly suspect that this process of domestication
had gone on for a considerable period. And it is commonly believed
that Sirach spoke for his colleagues when he identified wisdom and
law.[3] The process of this Israelite nationalization of wisdom has been
traced by Rylaarsdam[4] and does not call for additional treatment
here. But we would maintain, for reasons already seen, that prior to
the exile there existed a strong wisdom tradition among the Hebrews
and that this tradition remained relatively untouched in its essential
features by Yahwism. It influenced the prophetic and priestly traditions, but was little affected by them. This is not to say that the sage
was not then a member in good standing of the Covenant Community
and personally devoted to the community's God. But as we noted
earlier, the wise man was called upon to give good, practical counsel,
not to proclaim the religion of his people. If religious interests were
paramount to the sage, it is almost impossible to imagine his holding
his tongue in the face of the threats of idolatry and syncretism which
so exercised the great prophets. And yet, if there was such protest, we
have no evidence of it. We are convinced that the soundness of the
wise man's teaching was so undergirded by its self-authenticating
nature and by its connection with the learning of the ages, that he
felt no immediate need to make appeal to the sanctions of his Faith.
It was rather the representatives of religion who, seeing the value of
the wise man's teaching, felt called upon to incorporate much of it
into the structure of their thought and belief. The extent of theology's debt to philosophy is a perennial point of debate, but if the
debt has been gathering interest since Moses first drew upon the philosophy of Egypt and since Israel's priests and prophets borrowed from
their sagacious colleagues, it is perhaps not small. It would be a mistake, however, to stop here. For, as we have indicated, the religion of
Yahweh certainly did influence Israel's post-exilic wisdom. But since
it will appear that the major influence here was somewhat directly

2   Prov. 1:7.
3   Pfeiffer, *History . . .*, p. 384; Rylaarsdam, *Revelation . . .*, pp. 30-39.
4   *Op. cit.*, pp. 18-46.

linked to the presence of a skeptical spirit among the wise, we must go back and take special account of this less prominent mode of thought.

The observation that there existed among the ancient wise men both prudential and skeptical attitudes has become a truism. And yet if one looks closely for the relationship between these two attitudes, one notices something that is not quite so obvious: they existed frequently side by side in a kind of unresolved tension.

The ancient Babylonian proverbs, for all their assumption of man's ability to regulate his life and understand his world, yet include the following:

> Be you small or great, it is (your) god who is your support.[5]

> Will the early corn thrive? How can we know?
> Will the late corn thrive? How can we know? [6]

> The will of a god cannot be understood,
>   the way of a god cannot be known.
> Anything of a god (is difficult) to find out.[7]

Or, similarly, we find the same sense of the finitude of human knowledge in the Egyptian examples:

> Let not thy heart be puffed-up because of thy knowledge;
> Be not confident because thou art a wise man.
> Take counsel with the ignorant as well as the wise.
> The (full) limits of skill cannot be attained,
> And there is no skilled man equipped to his (full) advantage.[8]

> Do not spend the night fearful of the morrow.
> At daybreak what is the morrow like?
> God is (always) in his success,
> Whereas man is in his failure;
> One thing are the words which men say,
> Another is that which the god does.[9]

---

5   Lambert, *op. cit.*, p. 232.
6   *Op. cit.*, p. 250.
7   *Op. cit.*, p. 266.
8   *Instruction of the Vizier Ptahhotep,* Pritchard, *Texts,* p. 412.
9   *Instruction of Amenemopet*, Pritchard, *Texts,* p. 423.

The same spirit obtains in some of the biblical proverbs. Von Rad cites the following:[10]

> A man's mind plans his way,
>   but the LORD directs his steps.[11]

> Many are the plans of the mind of a man,
>   but it is the purpose of the LORD that will be established.[12]

> Every way of a man is right in his own eyes,
>   but the LORD weighs the heart.[13]

> A man's steps are ordered by the LORD;
>   how then can man understand his way?[14]

> No wisdom, no understanding, no counsel,
>   can avail against the LORD.
> The horse is made ready for the day of battle,
>   but the victory belongs to the LORD.[15]

The "words of Agur" in Prov. 30:2-4 display a similar attitude:

> Surely I am too stupid to be a man.
> I have not the understanding of a man.
> I have not learned wisdom,
>   nor have I knowledge of the Holy One.
> Who has ascended to heaven and come down?
> Who has gathered the wind in his fists?
> Who has wrapped up the waters in a garment?
> Who has established all the ends of the earth?
> What is his name, and what is his son's name?
> Surely you know!

If we move beyond the lore of proverbs, moreover, we encounter several well-known skeptical treatises, each dealing in its own way with the tension between the prudential, humanistic spirit and its

10   von Rad, *op. cit.*, p. 439.
11   Prov. 16:9.
12   Prov. 19:21.
13   Prov. 21:2.
14   Prov. 20:24.
15   Prov. 21:30-31.

skeptical counterpart, cognizant of the fundamental mystery which constitutes the boundary of man's intellectual capacities. From ancient Babylonia we have *Man and His God,* dating perhaps from as early as 2000 B.C.[16] We also have the so-called *Babylonian Job,* [17] *A Pessimistic Dialogue Between Master and Servant,* [18] and *A Dialogue About Human Misery.* [19] From Egypt we have *A Dispute Over Suicide.* [20] And in the Bible the skeptical side of wisdom is represented by Job and Ecclesiastes.

In all these works there is a sense of frustration concerning the ability of man to make sense out of his life. Although the problem of innocent (or relatively innocent) suffering is most often to the fore, it is not the suffering per se which is at issue, but its meaninglessness. It mocks and offends the elemental sense of justice and order upon which wisdom is based. But it may sometimes be the ambivalent character of all human decision which plagues the sage, as in the Babylonian *A Pessimistic Dialogue Between Master and Servant.* Or it may be the ultimate futility of man's striving in the face of his eventual annihilation in death, as in Ecclesiastes. But whatever the occasion for such skepticism, at the heart of it all is the honest recognition that despite man's great ability to order and structure and understand his life, there exists at the center of it all an impenetrable Mystery.

It is a mistake, we believe, to speak here of a 'skeptical tradition' and a 'prudential tradition' as though every old wise man represented either the one or the other. It greatly oversimplifies things to contrast the credulous and not-very-bright 'orthodox' sage with his more profound but 'heterodox' challenger. Three objections must be raised to such a picture, popular though it may be: First of all, one wonders how many times and in how many places the skeptic's caveat would need to be made before the simple brethren would 'catch on'. The fact is that almost as far back as we can go both moods are to be seen, and there is little if any 'progress' to be noted. Secondly, the character of wisdom, as revealed especially in proverbs, is not such as

16 Kramer, " 'Man and His God': . . .", p. 170.
17 Pritchard, *Texts,* pp. 434-37.
18 *Op. cit.,* pp. 437-38.
19 *Op. cit.,* pp. 438-40.
20 *Op. cit.,* pp. 405-07.

to demand absolute consistency.[21] We can no more demand of the aphorist that he reconcile every maxim with every other than we can insist that the poet reconcile his eloquent celebration of love's ever-lastingness with some later poetic agonizing over its transitoriness. And the wise man, we believe, stood solidly in a tradition which everywhere cultivated the proverb, and which consequently recognized and accepted the paradoxes of 'existential truth'. The fact is that the truths we know most deeply often contradict one another, and if we require that the ancient wise man be consistent in his treatment of them, we request of him more than we can legitimately ask of ourselves. In the third place, the proverb, which is so often cited as expressive of the 'prudential tradition', not only expresses occasional skeptical sentiments, but is itself frequently employed by the skeptics. Koheleth often uses forms reflective of the maxim,[22] and also makes use of proverbs themselves, not only to express prudential insights, but also as the vehicles of his skepticism:

> What is crooked cannot be made straight,
> and what is lacking cannot be numbered.[23]

> For in much wisdom is much vexation,
> and he who increases knowledge increases sorrow.[24]

> What gain has the worker from his toil?[25]

Job uses proverbs somewhat freely, and his poetry seems to owe much of its form to the aphoristic tradition. Furthermore, we have noted the use of proverbs in non-Israelite skeptical writings.[26]

It is much better, it would seem, to speak of the prudential and skeptical sentiments as existing in tension with one another rather than to think in terms of variant traditions. Surely some sages were of more gloomy temperament than others, and some undoubtedly displayed a generally cheerful approach to life's problems. But most, we

21   Above, pp. 69-70.
22   Above, pp. 85-88.
23   Eccles. 1:15.
24   Eccles. 1:18.
25   Eccles. 3:9.
26   See *I Will Praise the Lord of Wisdom* and *A Pessimistic Dialogue Between Master and Servant,* discussed above on page 58.

cannot but believe, would have affirmed both the ability of man to understand and control his world on the one hand, and his inability to comprehend it fully on the other.

But more must be said. For just as we are not content merely to observe and describe the antinomies of human existence, so neither were all the wise men of ancient times. They knew the tension, and they sought to resolve it; and it is in the more extended skeptical treatises that we find the various attempts at this resolution. If it was enough for the aphorist, or for the compiler of maxims, simply to set down contradictory proverbs and let it go at that, there were other spirits for whom this was not satisfactory. And if we examine some of their works we can see how they attempted to reconcile what they knew to be true according to human wisdom with what they knew to be true about the ultimate frustration of man's understanding.

Some of wisdom's skeptics dealt with the problem by insisting upon a dogmatic solution. The difficulty, they suggest, is only apparent. It only seems, at times, that the way of God — or of the gods — with man are unjust or beyond human understanding. If we but hold on to 'orthodoxy', making of it an absolute dogma, then eventually our faithfulness will be vindicated. To be sure, the tension is resolved between the humanist and skeptical insights, but at the expense of absolutizing the prudential claims in the face of contravening evidence. Or, to put it another way, the tension is 'resolved' by the denial of the claims of one of the elements in the tension.

We do not appear to have any clear ancient examples of this 'solution'; perhaps most sages were too much devoted to truth to entertain it seriously. But that it was held by some seems clear from the polemic intent of Job. One can hardly help but feel that the poet is countering some very real dogmatic claims as he pictures the stubborn three friends, so unwilling to abandon their rigid position. They seem to be caricatures of those who have so elevated the doctrine of rewards and punishments that they now see all suffering as presumptive evidence of unrighteousness. Even Job himself does not deny the principle of punishments and rewards, but in fact calls God to account on the basis of it. And when Bildad states the principle in chapter eight, Job replies, "Truly I know it is so: But how can a man be just before God?" [27] Here is the basic tension in one brief verse: Job does

27   Job 9:2.

not doubt man's wisdom (his knowledge of the doctrine of retribution), but neither can he blink the facts which seem to deny it. In his case it does not hold! It is not therefore always applicable! [28]

At the opposite pole from the dogmatists are the nihilists. For them life is beyond all understanding and embodies no trustworthy principles at all. Far from elevating principle to dogma, this 'solution' denies the principle altogether. Here we have a kind of dogmatism in reverse — making the vanity of all human wisdom the fundamental assumption. Once again, the tension is eliminated simply by denying one of its constitutive elements.

Exemplifying this approach is the Babylonian *A Pessimistic Dialogue Between Master and Servant*. [29] This work focuses upon the problem of the good, in the sense of profitable, human action; and it arrives at no happy conclusion. Each time the master proposes a course of action, his servant endorses its advisability with good reason. And when the master then decides upon an opposite course, the servant endorses that also with equally good reason. The unavoidable conclusion is that it is simply beyond human possibility to decide what is good and what is not good for a man to do. As Stamm has commented, the dialogue arrives at a skepticism which denies life. [30]

Exuding a similar despairing spirit is the Egyptian *A Dispute Over Suicide*. [31] Purporting to be a conversation between a man and his soul, it pictures life as not worth the living. All men are, it says, wicked; and even one's family and friends cannot be trusted. Although death is anticipated as is a recovery after illness, life here on earth is full to the brim with wicked deceit: "The gentle man has perished, (but) the violent man has access to everybody." [32]

---

[28]   H.H. Rowley writes of the principle of individual rewards and punishments that "as one of the great principles of the universe, this is undeniably sound. It only becomes mischievous when it is elevated into a hard and invariable law, so that suffering is believed to be the proof of sin." H.H. Rowley, *Submission in Suffering and Other Essays on Eastern Thought* (Cardiff: University of Wales Press, 1951), p. 3.

[29]   Pritchard, *Texts*, pp. 437-38.

[30]   Johann Jakob Stamm, *Das Leiden des Unschuldigen in Babylon und Israel* (*Abhandlungen zur Theologie des Alten und Neuen Testaments*) (Zurich: Zwingli-Verlag, 1946), p. 16. See also Zimmerli, *Die Weisheit . . .*, p. 35.

[31]   Pritchard, *Texts*, pp. 405-07.

[32]   *Op. cit.*, p. 406. See Zimmerli, *Die Weisheit . . .*, p. 35. While not of the

A third way of dealing with the tension is the way taken by Kohe-leth: acceptance of it in a spirit of resignation. [33] We have already noted that a number of 'conventional' proverbs are to be found in Ecclesiastes. [34] But at the same time the dominant theme of the book is the ultimate vanity of human existence. Wise and foolish must both die; the pleasures of life are transitory; man's labors are often for naught. There is, to be sure, validity in the prudential maxims of antiquity; but it is a limited validity. The goals of sagacious living are real, but only temporary. [35] We do best, we are told, by living accord-ing to wise counsel, making the most of what life has to offer, but resigning ourselves to the futility of attempting to make any enduring sense out of it.

Still a fourth way to deal with the dilemma can be called the way of faith. This is like the way of resignation in that it refuses to blink the reality of the tension, but different in that it directs man's life toward the divine realm from which help may come. Here we may cite a couple of Babylonian works: *I Will Praise the Lord of Wisdom* (the 'Babylonian Job') and *A Dialogue About Human Misery.*

The personal complaint of the former reminds us of Job. The narra-tor has been faithful in his religious duties, but his suffering has been great and there is no understanding of the divine purpose. Still, the lamenter has faith; and at last his trust is justified and Marduk heals him.

In *A Dialogue About Human Misery* a Job-like sufferer, in dialogue with a pious companion, complains of his undeserved torment and testifies to his former religious faithfulness. Yet his companion sug-gests that he has not been so faithful in his religious obligations, and urges him to return to them. When the sufferer goes on to complain of widespread injustice in the lives of others, his friend admits this seem-ing injustice and the impossibility of understanding it. Finally the

---

same genre, the Egyptian *A Song of the Harper* reflects the same general spirit. Pritchard, *Texts*, p. 467.

33   Zimmerli, *Die Weisheit . . .* , p. 36.

34   Above, pp. 85-88.

35   See Gordis, *op. cit.*, pp. 98-99. See also H.L. Ginsberg, "The Structure and Contents of the Book of Koheleth", *Wisdom in Israel and in the Ancient Near East,* eds. H.H. Rowley, Martin Noth, D. Winton Thomas (= Supplements to *Vetus Testamentum*, Vol. III) (Leiden: E.J. Brill, 1960), pp. 145-48.

sufferer appears to turn to the gods for mercy, following the counsel of his friend. The theoretical problems posed by the sufferer are not solved. He never learns why he must suffer or why injustice so often prevails. But "die Gewissheit der göttlichen Hilfe in naher Zukunft ist wichtiger als die Lösung des Rätsels, warum den A in seinem bisherigen Leben trotz seiner Frömmigkeit soviel Leid getroffen."[36]

A similar theme is found in the Sumerian *Man and His God*, dating perhaps from as early as 2000 B.C.[37] Although the doctrine of rewards and punishments was held by the ancient Sumerians, the writer of this work describes a case in which suffering is not to be seen as clearly justified. And according to the teaching of the work, "the victim has but one valid and effective recourse, and that is to continually glorify his god and keep wailing and lamenting before him until he turns a favourable ear to his prayers."[38] The victim of the piece, his health and wealth suddenly taken from him, does just that. And when his prayers at last are heeded, he is restored to his former happy estate.[39]

The theme of the faithful sufferer is most familiar to readers of the Bible from the prologue and epilogue of Job, and perhaps from chapters 27 and 28 as well.[40] In fact the theme of a righteous man who suffers as a result of the machinations of divine beings while remaining faithful through it all seems to be common in the ancient East. The Indian story of Hariscandra is well known, and a similar narrative has been noted among the Suahelis.[41]

But there is yet another way of dealing with this tension, and this is the way of Job as he is depicted in the poetic portion of the book.

---

36 Stamm, *op. cit.*, p. 24.
37 Kramer, "Man and . . . ", p. 170.
38 *Op. cit.*, p. 171.
39 *Op. cit.*, pp. 170-82.
40 See Hillel A. Fine, "The Tradition of a Patient Job", *Journal of Biblical Literature*, Vol. LXXIV (March, 1955), pp. 28-32.
41 Terrien, "The Book . . . ", p. 879. The origin of the prose material of Job is a much discussed problem, too complex to be entered into here. However, for an arresting study which claims to discern an ancient legend going back perhaps to 1200 B.C., see Georg Fohrer, "Überlieferung und Wandlung der Hioblegende", *Festschrift Friedrich Baumgärtel (Erlanger Forschungen*, Reihe A: *Geisteswissenschaften*, Band 10) (Erlangen: Für den Druck herausgegeben von Leonard Rost, 1959), pp. 48-53.

The poem is too well known to be sketched here, but it must be noted that in the climactic words of Job 42:5 a new and definitive answer is given to the humanism-skepticism tension:

> I had heard of thee by the hearing of the ear,
> but now my eye sees thee.

Just as with the other answers, no solution to the theoretical problem of God's justice is forthcoming. But now we meet something new: a dimension of life which is peculiarly Hebrew. For all his indebtedness to international wisdom, the poet was also a true child of Israel, and shows this in Job's meeting with God.

For it is in the *encounter* that the historical Faith of Israel shines through. Israel's God is not isolated and unapproachable; he is not to be dealt with solely through the operation of the priestly cult. He is One who meets his children in the intimacy of the Covenant.

Hiob hört das Wort, durch welches Mose und die Propheten berufen wurden, und welches sie als Botschaft dem Volke auszurichten hatten . . . Nur in Israel gibt es nach dem Zeugnis der besprochenen Werke eine Realität, welche mit Religion und Kultus nichts zu tun hat. Wir meinen die Offenbarung des personhaften Herrn, die den Leidenden in ein neues Verhältnis zum göttlichen Willen bringt.[42]

As in other cultures, Israel's sages knew man's frailty and limitation. But Israel alone knew Him who was their Creator and who stood at the boundary of all human understanding. The Hebrew wise man, at least as we meet him in Job, was indebted not only to his own international tradition, but to the great realities of Israel's election and her prophetic witness to God's active participation in the affairs of man.

The tension, to be sure, is not here resolved, but we may suggest that in the man-God relationship reflected in Job it is given a new stability. Man need not deny his own experience in a desperate ortho-

---

[42] Stamm, *op. cit.*, pp. 80-81. See also Emil G. Kraeling, *The Book of the Ways of God* (New York: Charles Scribner's Sons, 1939), p. 15; Georg Fohrer, *Das Buch Job* ("Kommentar zum Alten Testament," Vol. XVI) (Gütersloher Verlagshaus Gerd Mohn, 1963), p. 47; Robinson, *Job . . .*, p. 123; Walther Eichrodt, 'Vorsehungsglaube und Theodizee im Alten Testament", *Festschrift Otto Procksch* (Leipzig: A. Deichert, 1934), pp. 67-68.

doxy; he need not despair of any purpose in life; he need not resign himself to an unknown fate; he need not content himself with a blind trust in the inscrutable economy of Providence. He can affirm the truth of ancient prudence along with the truth of man's finitude and God's ultimate mystery — affirm these truths in all their contradictoriness because he knows the One who stands above and beyond the polarities of man's experience.[43]

The proverb, then, was not simply an expression of 'prudential wisdom' which then had its naïveté exposed by its skeptical critics. It, too, sometimes expressed skeptical attitudes, and was not infrequently pressed into literary service by the skeptical writers themselves. When it assumed a more optimistic and confident posture, as it most frequently did, it was not thereby standing in total opposition to the skeptics, unless of course it was used to express an unyielding dogma. The prudence of proverbs is more properly understood to have existed in tension with the more skeptical sentiments. A wisdom restricted to prudence alone would not have been true to the total experience of man. But a wisdom which had room only for skepticism would have been equally distorting. Both affirmed what man knew to be true. And it was the task of some of wisdom's greatest minds to attempt resolutions of this basic tension.

---

[43] Perhaps Humbert is saying much the same thing when he says that the question in Job is that of divine justice versus human justice. But we cannot agree with him that the claims of human justice are there invalidated. Job knows full well the frailty of human reason and the incomprehensibility of the ways of God, as is clear from 9:1ff. But if human justice could make no claims at all the book would be rather pointless. Job's claims would finally appear to be hardly more than vain histrionics. See Paul Humbert, "Le Modernisme de Job", *Wisdom in Israel and in the Ancient Near East*, eds. H.H. Rowley, Martin Noth, D. Winton Thomas (= Supplements to *Vetus Testamentum*, Vol. III) (Leiden: E.J. Brill, 1960), pp. 150-61, especially pp. 160-61.

SUMMARY

The object of our work has been to set forth the reasons for the inclination among many Bible scholars to underrate the value of the proverbs of the Old Testament, and to investigate three of these reasons in a somewhat detailed manner.

We have noted six reasons for the present eclipse of biblical proverbs: (1) Proverbs in general no longer enjoy the popularity in our culture which was once theirs. (2) Proverbs, because of their arresting form, are subject to such overuse that they soon become trite. (3) Most of the biblical examples are found in the book of Proverbs, and the reading of such disconnected collection of independent maxims soon becomes tedious. (4) We fail to appreciate the form of the biblical proverb. (5) We do not understand the function of this form in ancient Israel. And (6) the biblical skeptics appear to vitiate the optimistic, prudential spirit of most of the proverb literature. Since the last three reasons seemed to call for further investigation, we devoted the major portion of our work to this task.

We examined the form and function of proverbs in general and of proverbs in the ancient Near East and in Israel. In the light of this examination we then attempted to assess the proverb's importance in Hebrew life and thought and in relation to skeptical wisdom, which so frequently seems to be at odds with it.

It was concluded that the form of the proverb is frequently poetic, and that it is best understood 'poetically'. It was further shown that the function of the proverb is best understood as 'philosophical', and that it is commonly used to instruct, to entertain, and to preserve legal tradition. The proverb, so understood, was found to have been prevalent throughout the ancient Near East and in ancient Israel.

We fail to appreciate the form of these ancient maxims because their poetic flavor is lost in translation, and their usage is not always immediately clear. When we sought out their probable use in ancient times, several observations were made: Educational usage was found to have been universal throughout the ancient Near East. As entertainment, parallel proverb stichs may have been used in a kind of 'proverb-riddle' game lying behind the development of the primitive one-line maxim into the familiar biblical distich. This phenomenon, it was suggested, may even point to the genesis of the parallel poetic form. Legal usage was best seen in the second person moral injunctions of ancient Near Eastern wisdom, the Egyptian examples approaching to something very close to divine commandments.

In assessing the proverb's influence upon Hebrew culture, we have argued that there is clear evidence of its influence upon both the prophetic and the priestly traditions. The prophets seem to have used many proverbs in their proclamations, and ethically they appear to have been dependent upon ancient wisdom teaching. The priestly tradition seems to have been influenced by proverbs at two points. The wisdom psalms appear to show dependence upon this genre of wisdom teaching, and Israel's apodictic law apparently derives from the maxims of Egyptian wisdom.

Skeptical and prudential wisdom are seen to have existed in tension with each other from very ancient times, the prudential proverbs simply reflecting one element in that tension, with certain proverbs standing in contrast to them. Of a number of attempts to deal with this tension, Job reflects a peculiarly Hebrew understanding, an understanding which suffers the tension to stand finally unresolved.

BIBLIOGRAPHY

BOOKS

Albright, William Foxwell, *Archeology and the Religion of Israel* (Baltimore: Johns Hopkins Press, 1942).

—, *From Stone Age to Christianity*, 2d ed. (Baltimore: Johns Hopkins Press, 1946).

Anderson, Bernard W., *Understanding the Old Testament* (Englewood Cliffs, New Jersey: Prentice-Hall, Inc., 1957).

Anthes, Rudolph, *Lebensregeln und Lebensweisheit der alten Ägypter* (=*Der Alte Orient*, 32 Band/Heft 2) (Leipzig: J.C. Hinrichs'sche Buchhandlung, 1933).

Baab, Otto J., *The Theology of the Old Testament* (New York and Nashville: Abingdon-Cokesbury Press, 1949).

Baikie, James, *A History of Egypt*, Vol. I (New York: The Macmillan Co., 1929).

Baldwin, Edward Chauncey, *Types of Literature in the Old Testament* (New York: Thomas Nelson and Sons, 1929).

Baron, Salo W., *A Social and Religious History of the Jews*, Vol. 1 (New York: Columbia University Press, 1952).

Barr, James, *The Semantics of Biblical Language* (London: Oxford University Press, 1961).

Barton, George Aaron, *A Critical and Exegetical Commentary on the Book of Ecclesiastes* (*The International Critical Commentary*) (New York: Charles Scribner's Sons, 1909).

Baumgärtel, D. Friedrick, *Der Hiobdialogue: Aufriss und Deutung* (=*Beiträge zur Wissenschaft von Alten und Neuen Testament*, Vierte Folge, Heft 9), (Stuttgart: W. Kohlhammer Verlag, 1933).

Baumgartner, Walter, *Israelitische und altorientalische Weisheit* (Tübingen: J.C.B. Mohr, 1933).

Beebe, H. Keith, *The Old Testament, An Introduction to Its Literary, Historical, and Religious Traditions* (Belmont, California: Dickenson Publishing Company, Inc., 1970).

Bentzen, Aage, *Introduction to the Old Testament*, 2 vols., 6th ed. (Copenhagen: G.E.C. Gad Publisher, 1961).

Bertholet, Alfred, *A History of Hebrew Civilization,* trans. A.K. Dallas (London: George G. Harrap & Company Ltd., 1926).

Bettan, Israel, *The Five Scrolls: A Commentary on the Song of Songs, Ruth, Lamentations, Ecclesiastes, Esther* (Cincinnati: Union of American Hebrew Congregations, 1950).

Bewer, Julias A., *The Literature of the Old Testament,* 3d ed. rev. Emil G. Kraeling (New York: Columbia University Press, 1962).

Boman, Thorlief, *Hebrew Thought Compared With Greek,* trans. Jules L. Moreau (London: SCM Press Ltd., 1960).

Bone, Robert G., *Ancient History* (=*New Students Outline Series*) (Ames, Iowa: Littlefield, Adams & Company, 1955).

Breasted, James Henry, *The Dawn of Conscience* (New York: Charles Scribner's Sons, 1934).

—, *Development of Religion and Thought in Ancient Egypt* (New York: Charles Scribner's Sons, 1912).

Bright, John, *A History of Israel* (Philadelphia: Westminster Press, 1959).

Brown, Francis; Samuel Rolles Driver; Charles A. Briggs, *A Hebrew and English Lexicon of the Old Testament,* rev. ed. (Oxford: At the Clarendon Press, 1957).

Brunner, Hellmut, *Altägyptische Erziehung* (Wiesbaden: Otto Harrosowitz, 1957).

Burrows, Millar, *An Outline of Biblical Theology* (Philadelphia: The Westminster Press, 1946).

—, *What Mean These Stones?* (New Haven: American Schools of Oriental Research, 1941).

Cassirer, Ernst, *Language and Myth,* trans. Susanne K. Langer (New York: Harper & Brothers, 1946).

Champion, Selwyn Gurney, *Racial Proverbs* (New York: The Macmillan Company, 1938).

Cheyne, Thomas Kelly, *Job and Solomon: or the Wisdom of the Old Testament* (London: Kegan Paul, Trench & Co., 1887).

Childs, Brevard, S., *Memory and Tradition in Israel* (=*Studies in Biblical Theology,* No. 37) (London: SCM Press, 1962).

Cohen, Abraham, *Proverbs* (Hindhead, Surrey: Soncino Press, 1954).

Creelman, Harlan, *An Introduction to the Old Testament Chronologically Arranged* (New York: The Macmillan Company, 1917).

Culler, Arthur J., *Creative Religious Literature* (New York: The Macmillan Company, 1930).

Danquah, J.B., *The Akan Doctrine of God* (London and Redhill: Lutterworth Press, 1944).

Davidson, Andrew Bruce, *The Book of Job, With Notes, Introduction and Appendix* (*The Cambridge Bible for Schools and Colleges*) (Cambridge: At the University Press, 1884).

—, *The Theology of the Old Testament* (New York: Charles Scribner's Sons, 1904).

Davison, W.T., *The Wisdom-Literature of the Old Testament* (London: Charles H. Kelly, 1894).

Dijk, J.J.A. van, *La Sagesse Suméro-Accadienne* (= *Commentationes Orientales*, Nederlandsch Instituut Voor Het Nabije Oosten, Vol 1) (Leiden: E.J. Brill, 1953).

Doke, Clement M., *Lamba Folk-Lore* (=*Memoirs of the American Folk-Lore Society*, Vol. 20) (New York: The American Folk-lore Society, 1927).

Driver, Godfrey Rolles, *Semitic Writing from Pictograph to Alphabet*, rev. ed. (*The Schweich Lectures of the British Academy*, 1944) (London: Oxford University Press, 1944).

Driver, Samuel Rolles, *An Introduction to the Literature of the Old Testament*, 10th ed. rev. & enlarged (*International Theological Library*) (New York: Charles Scribner's Sons, 1902).

Driver, Samuel Rolles and George Buchanan Gray, *A Critical and Exegetical Commentary on the Book of Job*, Vol. I (The International Critical Commentary) (New York: Charles Scribner's Sons, 1921).

Dubarle, O.P., *Les Sages d'Israël* (Paris: Les Éditions du Cerf, 1946).

Duesberg, Hilaire, *Les Scribes Inspirés*, 2 vols. (Paris: Desclée de Brouwer, 1938-39).

Eichrodt, Walther, *Man in the Old Testament*, trans. K. and R. Gregor Smith (London: SCM Press, 1951).

—, *Theology of the Old Testament*, Vol. I, trans. J.A. Baker (Philadelphia: The Westminster Press, 1961).

Eissfeldt, Otto, *Der Maschal im Alten Testament* (=*Beihefte* zur *Zeitschrift für die alttestamentliche Wissenschaft*, Vol. XXIV) (Giesen: Verlag von Alfred Töpelmann, 1913).

—, *Einleitung in das Alte Testament* (=*Neue Theologische Grundrisse*, 3., neubearbeitete Auflage) (Tübingen: J.C.B. Mohr (Paul Siebeck), 1964).

Elmslie, William A.L., *Studies in Life from Jewish Proverbs* (London: James Clark & Co., 1917).

Erman, Adolph, *The Literature of the Ancient Egyptians: Poems, Narratives, and Manuals of Instruction from the Third and Second Millennia B.C.*, trans. Aylward M. Blackman (London: Methuen & Co., 1927).

Fichtner, Johannes, *Die altorientalische Weisheit in ihrer israelitisch-jüdischen Ausprägung: Eine Studie zur Nationalizierung der Weisheit in Israel* (=*Beihefte* zur *Zeitschrift für die alttestamentliche Wissenschaft*, No. 62) (Giessen: A. Töpelmann, 1933).

—, *Weisheit Salomos* (=*Handbuch zum Alten Testament*, 2, Reihe 6) (Tübingen: J.C.B. Mohr (Paul Siebeck), 1938).

Fohrer, Georg, *Das Buch Job* (=*Kommentar zum Alten Testament*, Vol. XVI) (Gütersloher Verlagshaus Gerd Mohn, 1963).

Fowler, Henry Thatcher, *A History of the Literature of Ancient Israel* (New York: The Macmillan Co., 1912).

Frankfort, Henry, *Kingship and the Gods* (Chicago: University of Chicago Press, 1948).

Franklin, Benjamin, *The Autobiography of Benjamin Franklin, Poor Richard's Almanac, and Other Papers* (*The Home Library*) (New York: A.L. Burt, n.d.).

Gardiner, J.H., *The Bible as English Literature* (New York: Charles Scribner's Sons, 1906).

Gemser, Berend, *Sprüche Salomos* (Tübingen: J.C.B. Mohr, 1937).

Genung, John Franklin, *The Hebrew Literature of Wisdom in the Light of To-day* (Boston and New York: Houghton, Mifflin and Company, 1906).

Gerstenberger, Erhard, *Wesen und Herkunft des 'Apodiktischen Rechts'* (=*Wissenschaftliche Monographien zum Alten und Neuen Testament*, Vol. XX) (Neukirchen-Vluyn: Neukirchen Verlag, 1965).

Gese, Hartmut, *Lehre und Wirklichkeit in der Alten Weisheit* (Tübingen: J.C.B. Mohr (Paul Siebeck), 1958).

Ginsberg, H. Louis, *Studies in Koheleth* (=*Texts and Studies of the Jewish Theological Seminary of America*, Vol. XVII) (New York: The Jewish Theological Seminary of America, 1950).

Goettsberger, J., *Einleitung in das Alte Testament* (Freiburg im Breisgau: Herder & Co. G.M.B.H. Verlagsbuchhandlung, 1928).

Gordis, Robert, *Koheleth – The Man and His World*, 2d ed., augmented (New York: Bloch Publishing Co. for The Jewish Theological Seminary of America, 1955).

—, *The Wisdom of Koheleth: A New Translation with a Commentary and an Introductory Essay* (London: East and West Library, 1950).

Gordon, Cyrus H., *Before the Bible* (New York: Harper & Row, 1962).

Gordon, Edmund I., *Sumerian Proverbs: Glimpses of Everyday Life in Ancient Mesopotamia* (Philadelphia: The University Museum, 1959).

Gottwald, Norman K., *A Light to the Nations* (New York: Harper & Brothers, 1959).

Gray, George Buchanan, *A Critical Introduction to the Old Testament* (New York: Charles Scribner's Sons, 1913).

—, *The Forms of Hebrew Poetry* (London: Hodder & Stoughton, 1915).

Gregg, J.A.F., *The Wisdom of Solomon* (*The Cambridge Bible for Schools and Colleges*) (Cambridge: At the University Press, 1909).

Gressmann, Hugo, *Israels Spruchweisheit im Zusammenhang der Weltliteratur* (Berlin: Karl Curtius, 1925).

Guinzbourg, V.S.M. de, ed., *Wit and Wisdom of the United Nations* (New York: V.S.M. de Guinzbourg, 1961).

Gunn, Battiscombe, *The Instruction of Ptah-hotep and \ the Instruction of Ke'gemni*, 2d ed. (London: John Murray, 1912).

Harper, William Rainey, *The Work of the Old Testament Priests* (Chicago: The University of Chicago Press, 1908).

—, *The Work of the Old Testament Sages* (Chicago: The American Institute of Sacred Literature , 1904).

Harrelson, Walter, *Interpreting the Old Testament* (New York: Holt, Rinehart and Winston, Inc., 1964).

Hempel, Johannes, *Althebräische Literatur und ihre hellenistisch-jüdisches Nachlaben* (=*Handbuch der Literaturwissenschaft*, Vol. II) (Wildpark-Potsdam: Akademische Verlagsgesellschaft Athenaion M.B.H., 1930).

Henshaw, Thomas, *The Writings: The Third Division of the Old Testament Canon* (London: George Allen & Unwin Ltd., 1963).

Hermisson, Hans-Jürgen, *Studien zur Israelitischen Spruchweisheit* (=*Wissenschaftliche Monographien zum Alten und Neuen Testament*, Vol. XXVIII) (Neukirchen-Vluyn: Neukirchener Verlag, 1968).

Herskovits, Melville J. and Frances S., *Dahomean Narrative: A Cross-Cultural Analysis* (=*Northwestern University African Studies*, No. 1) (Evanston, Ill.: Northwestern University Press, 1958).

Hertzberg, Hans Wilhelm, *Der Prediger* (*Kommentar zum Alten Testament*, Vol. XVII, Part 4) (Gütersloher Verlagshaus Gerd Mohn, 1963).

Heschel, Abraham J., *The Prophets* (New York: Harper & Row, 1962).

Hölscher, Gustav, *Geschichte der israelitischen und jüdischen Religion* (Geissen: Verlag von Alfred Töpelmann, 1922).

Humbert, Paul, *Recherches sur les sources égyptiennes de la littérature sapientale d'Israël* (Neuchâtel Secrétariat de l'Université, 1929).

Irwin, William A., *The Old Testament: Keystone of Human Culture* (New York: Henry Schuman, 1952).

Jacob, Edmund, *Theology of the Old Testament*, trans. Arthur W. Heathcote and Philip J. Allcock (New York: Harper & Brothers, 1958).

James, Fleming, *Personalities of the Old Testament* (*The Hale Lectures*, 1938) (New York: Charles Scribner's Sons, 1939).

Jastrow, Morris, *A Gentle Cynic, Being a Translation of the Book of Koheleth, Commonly Known as Ecclesiastes, Stripped of Later Additions; Also Its Origin, Growth and Interpretation* (Philadelphia: J.B. Lippincott Company, 1919).

Kelsen, Hans, *Society and Nature* (Chicago: The University of Chicago Press, 1943).

Kent, Charles Foster, *The Makers and Teachers of Judaism* (New York: Charles Scribner's Sons, 1911).

—, *The Wise Men of Ancient Israel and Their Proverbs* (Boston: Silver, Burdett & Company, 1895).

Kent, Charles Foster and Millar Burrows, *Proverbs and Didactic Poems* (New York: Charles Scribner's Sons, 1927).

Kittel, Rudolph, *Geschichte des Volkes Israel*, Vol. III (Stuttgart: W. Kohlhammer, 1929).

—, *The Religion of the People of Israel*, trans. R. Caryl Micklem (New York: The Macmillan Co., 1925).

Köhler, Ludwig, *Old Testament Theology*, trans. A.L. Todd (Philadelphia: Westminster Press, 1957).

Kraeling, Emil G., *The Book of the Ways of God* (New York : Charles Scribner's Sons, 1939).

Kramer, Samuel Noah, *From the Tablets of Sumer* (Indian Hills, Colorado: Falcon's Wing Press, 1956).

—, *The Sumerians: Their History, Culture, and Character* (Chicago: The University of Chicago Press, 1963).

Kremer, Edmund P., *German Proverbs* (Stanford: Stanford University Press, 1955).

Kris, Ernst, *Psychoanalytic Explorations in Art* (New York: International Universities Press, Inc., 1952).

Kroeber, Alfred L., *Anthropology* (New York: Harcourt, Brace and Company, 1923).

Lambert, W.G., *Babylonian Wisdom Literature* (Oxford: At the Clarendon Press, 1960).

Langdon, Stephen, *Babylonian Wisdom* (London: Luzac & Co., 1923).

Leclercq, Jean, *The Love of Learning and the Desire for God*, trans. Catherine Misrahi (*A Mentor Omega Book*) (New York: New American Library, 1961).

Levy-Bruhl, Lucien, *How Natives Think*, trans. Lilian A. Clare (London: G. Allen & Unwin Ltd., 1926).

—, *Primitive Mentality*, trans. Lilian A. Clare (London: George Allen & Unwin Ltd., 1923).

Lindblom, Johannes, *Prophecy in Ancient Israel* (Philadelphia: Fortress Press, 1962).

Lowie, R.H., *Social Organization* (New York: Rinehart & Company, 1948).

McCasland, Selby Vernon, *The Religions of the Bible* (New York: Thomas Y. Crowell Company, 1960).

McCown, Chester C., *Man, Morals and History* (New York: Harper & Brothers, 1958).

Macdonald, Duncan Black, *The Hebrew Literary Genius* (Princeton: Princeton University Press, 1933).

—, *The Hebrew Philosophical Genius* (Princeton: Princeton University Press, 1936).

McFadyen, John Edgar, *Introduction to the Old Testament* (New York: Hodder & Stoughton, 1906).

McGlinchey, James M., *The Teaching of Amen-em-ope and the Book of Proverbs* (Washington D.C.: Catholic University of America Press, 1939).

McKane, William, *Prophets and Wise Men* (=*Studies in Biblical Theology*, No. 44) (London: SCM Press Ltd., 1965).

Martin, G. Currie, ed., *Proverbs, Ecclesiastes, and Song of Songs* (*The Century Bible*) (Edinburgh: T.C. & E.C. Jack, 1908).

Matthews, Isaac G., *The Religious Pilgrimage of Israel* (New York: Harper & Brothers, 1947).

Meinhold, Johannes, *Die Weisheit Israels in Sprüche, Sage, und Dichtung* (Leipzig: Quelle & Meyer, 1908).

Meissner, Bruno, *Die babylonisch-assyrische Literatur* (*Handbuch der Literaturwissenschaft*) (Wildpark-Potsdam: Akademische Verlagsgesellschaft Athenaion M.B.H., 1927-28).

—, *Babylonien und Assyrien*, Vol. II (Heidelberg: Carl Winters Universitätsbuchhandlung, 1925).

Metzger, Bruce M., *An Introduction to the Apocrypha* (New York: Oxford University Press, 1957).

Montefiore, Claude G., *Lectures on the Origin and Growth of Religion as Illustrated by the Religion of the Ancient Hebrews*, 3d ed. (*The Hibbert Lectures*, 1892) (London: Williams and Norgate, 1897).

Montgomery, James Alan, *Arabia and the Bible* (Philadelphia: University of Pennsylvania Press, 1934).

—, *A Critical and Exegetical Commentary on the Books of Kings*, ed. Henry Snyder Gehman (*The International Critical Commentary*) (New York: Charles Scribner's Sons, 1951).

Moore, George Foot, *The Literature of the Old Testament* (New York: Henry Holt & Co., 1913).

Moulton, Richard Green, *The Literary Study of the Bible* (Boston: D.C. Heath & Co., 1895).

–, *A Short Introduction to the Literature of the Bible* (Boston: D.C. Heath & Co., 1901).

Mowinckel, Sigmund, *The Psalms in Israel's Worship*, Vol. II, trans. D.R. Ap-Thomas (New York: Abingdon Press, 1962).

Muilenburg, James, *Specimens of Biblical Literature* (New York: Thomas Y. Crowell Company, 1923).

–, *The Way of Israel* (New York: Harper & Brothers, 1961).

Murphy, Roland Edward, *Seven Books of Wisdom* (Milwaukee: The Bruce Publishing Company, 1960).

Nielson, Eduard, *Oral Tradition* (= *Studies in Biblical Theology*, No. 11) (London: SCM Press, 1954).

Noth, Martin, *The History of Israel*, 2d ed., translation rev. by P.R. Ackroyd (New York: Harper & Brothers, 1960).

Noyes, C., *The Genius of Israel* (Boston and New York: Houghton Mifflin Co., 1924).

Oesterley, William O.E., *The Book of Proverbs* (New York: E.P. Dutton and Company Inc., 1929).

–, *The Wisdom of Egypt and the Old Testament* (London: S.P.C.K., 1927).

Oesterley, William O.E. and Theodore H. Robinson, *Hebrew Religion* (New York: The Macmillan Company, 1930).

–, *An Introduction to the Books of the Old Testament* (New York: The Macmillan Co., 1934).

Olmstead, Albert Ten Eyck, *History of Palestine and Syria to the Macedonian Conquest* (New York: Charles Scribner's Sons, 1931).

Paterson, John, *The Book that is Alive* (New York: Charles Scribner's Sons, 1954).

Peake, A.S., *Job: Introduction: Revised Version with Notes and Index* (*The Century Bible*) (Edinburgh: T.C. & E.C. Jack, 1904).

Pederson, Johannes, *Israel, Its Life and Culture*, 4 parts in 2 vols. (London: Oxford University Press, 1926-40).

Peet, T.E., *A Comparative Study of the Literatures of Egypt, Palestine and Mesopotamia* (*The Schweich Lectures*, 1929) (London: Oxford University Press, 1931).

Pfeiffer, Robert H., *History of New Testament Times, with an Introduction to the Apocrypha* (New York: Harper & Brothers, 1949).

–, *Introduction to the Old Testament* (New York: Harper & Brothers, 1948).

Power, A.D. *Ecclesiastes, or the Preacher* (London: Longmans, Green and Co., 1952).

Pritchard, James B., *The Ancient Near East in Pictures* (Princeton: Princeton University Press, 1954).

–, ed., *Ancient Near Eastern Texts*, 2d ed. (Princeton: Princeton University Press, 1955).

Rad, Gerhard von, *Old Testament Theology*, trans. D.M.G. Stalker, 2 vols. (Edinburgh and London: Oliver and Boyd, 1962 and 1965).

Radin, Paul, *Primitive Man as Philosopher*, rev. ed. (New York: Dover Publications, 1957).

Rankin, O.S., *Israel's Wisdom Literature* (Edinburgh: T. and T. Clark, 1936).

Ranston, Harry, *The Old Testament Wisdom Books and Their Teaching* (London: Epworth Press, 1930).

Richardson, Alan, ed. *A Theological Word Book of the Bible* (London: SCM Press, 1950).

Richter, W., *Recht und Ethos* (= *Studien zum Alten und Neuen Testament*, Vol. XV) (München: Kösel-Verlag, 1966).

Ringgren, Helmer, *Sprüche* (*Das Alte Testemant Deutsch*, Teilband 16/1) (Göttingen: Vandenhoeck & Ruprecht, 1962).

Robinson, H. Wheeler, *Inspiration and Revelation in the Old Testament* (New York: Oxford University Press, 1946).

Robinson, Theodore H., *Job and His Friends* (London: SCM Press Ltd., 1954).

—, *The Poetry of the Old Testament* (London: Duckworth, 1947).

Rowley, H.H., *The Faith of Israel* (London: SCM Press, 1956).

—, *Submission in Suffering and Other Essays on Eastern Thought* (Cardiff: University of Wales Press, 1951).

—, *The Unity of the Bible* (Philadelphia: Westminster Press, 1953).

Rylaarsdam, J. Coert, *Revelation in Jewish Wisdom Literature* (Chicago: The University of Chicago Press, 1946).

Sachs, Hans, *The Creative Unconscious* (Cambridge, Mass.: Sci-Art Publishers, 1942).

Sandmel, Samuel, *The Hebrew Scriptures* (New York: Alfred A. Knopf, 1963).

Schmid, Hans Heinrich, *Wesen und Geschichte der Weisheit: Eine Untersuchung zur Altorientalischen und Israelitischen Weisheitsliteratur* (Berlin: Verlag Alfred Töpelmann, 1966).

Schmidt, Johannes, *Studien zur Stilistik der alttestamentlichen Spruchliteratur* (=*Alttestamentliche Abhandlungen*, XIII. Band 1. Heft) (Münster: Verlag der Aschendorffschen Verlagsbuchhandlung, 1936).

Scott, R.B.Y., *Proverbs, Ecclesiastes* (=*The Anchor Bible*, Vol. XVIII) (Garden City, New York: Doubleday & Company, Inc., 1965).

—, *The Relevance of the Prophets* (New York: The Macmillan Company, 1957).

Sellin, Ernst, *Introduction to the Old Testament*, trans. W. Montgomery (London: Hodder and Stoughton Ltd., 1923).

Skladny, Udo, *Die ältesten Spruchsammlungen in Israel* (Göttingen: Vandenhoeck & Ruprecht, 1962).

Smith, Henry Preserved, *A Critical and Exegetical Commentary on the Books of Samuel* (*The International Critical Commentary*) (New York: Charles Scribner's Sons, 1902).

Snaith, Norman H, *The Distinctive Ideas of the Old Testament* (London: Epworth Press, 1944).

Sprau, George, *Literature in the Bible* (New York: The Macmillan Company, 1932).

Stamm, Johann Jakob, *Le Décalogue à la lumière des recherches contemporaines*, trans. Philippe Reymond (*Cahiers Théologiques*) (Neuchatel: Éditions Delachaux et Niestlé, 1959).

—, *Das Leiden des Unschuldigen in Babylon und Israel* (*Abhandlungen zur Theologie des Alten und Neuen Testaments*) (Zurich: Zwingli-Verlag, 1946).

Stevenson, Burton, ed., *The Home Book of Quotations* (New York: Dodd, Mead & Company, 1956).

Stevenson, William Barron, *The Poem of Job, A Literary Study with a New Translation* (*The Schweich Lectures of the British Academy*, 1943) (London: Oxford University Press, 1947).

Strahan, James, *The Book of Job Interpreted* (Edinburgh: T. & T. Clark, 1913).

Taylor, Archer, *The Proverb and an Index to the Proverb* (Hatboro, Pennsylvania: Folklore Associates; Copenhagen: Rosenkilde and Bagger, 1962).

Thurnwald, Richard, *Die Menschliche Gesellschaft* (Berlin: Walter de Gruyter & Co., 1931).

Toy, Crawford H., *A Critical and Exegetical Commentary on the Book of Proverbs* (*The International Critical Commentary*) (New York: Charles Scribner's Sons, 1899).

Tyciak, Julius, *Die Weisheitsbücher des Alten Testaments* (Paderborn: Ferdinand Schöningh Verlag, 1948).

Volz, Paul, *Der Geist Gottes und die verwandten Erscheinungen im Alten Testament und im anschliessenden Judentum* (Tübingen: J.C.B. Mohr (Paul Siebeck), 1910).

Vriezen, T.C., *An Outline of Old Testament Theology,* trans. S. Neuijen (Wageningen, Holland: H. Veenman & Zonen, 1958).

Weiser, Artur, *The Old Testament: Its Formation and Development,* trans. Dorothea M. Barton (New York: Association Press, 1961).

Welch, Adam C., *The Religion of Israel Under the Kingdom* (*The Kerr Lectures,* 1911-12) (Edinburgh: T. & T. Clark, 1912).

Whedbee, James William, *Isaiah and Wisdom*, Ph. D. Dissertation, Yale University, 1968 (Ann Arbor: University Microfilms, Inc., 1969).

Whybray, R.N., *Wisdom in Proverbs* (=*Studies in Biblical Theology,* No. 45) (London: SCM Press Ltd., 1965).

Wild, Laura H., *A Literary Guide to the Bible* (Garden City, New Jersey: Doubleday, Doran & Company, Inc., 1922).

Wilson, John A., *The Culture of Ancient Egypt* (*Phoenix Books*) (Chicago: The University of Chicago Press, 1951).

Wolff, Hans Walter, *Amos' Geistige Heimat* (= *Wissenschaftliche Monographien zum Alten und Neuen Testament*, Vol. XVIII) (Neukirchen-Vluyn: Neukirchener Verlag, 1964).

Wood, Irving F., *The Spirit of God in Biblical Literature* (New York: A.C. Armstrong & Son, 1904).

Wright, G. Ernest, *Biblical Archeology* (Philadelphia: The Westminster Press, 1957).

—, *God Who Acts* (=*Studies in Biblical Theology* No. 8) (London: SCM Press, 1952).

—, *The Old Testament Against Its Environment* (=*Studies in Biblical Theology*, No. 2) (London: SCM Press, 1950).

Wright, G. Ernest and Reginald H. Fuller, *The Book of the Acts of God* (Garden City, New Jersey: Doubleday, 1957).

Würthwein, Ernst, *Die Weisheit Ägyptens und das Alte Testament* (Marburg: N.G. Elwert Verlag, 1960).

Zimmerli, Walther, *Das Buch des Predigers Salomo* (=*Das Alte Testament Deutsch*, Teilband 16/1) (Göttingen: Vandenhoeck & Ruprecht, 1962).
—, *Die Weisheit des Predigers Salomo*, "Aus der Welt der Religion" (Berlin: Verlag von Alfred Töpelmann, 1936).

ARTICLES AND PERIODICALS

Albright, William Foxwell, "An Archaic Hebrew Proverb in an Amarna Letter from Central Palestine", *Bulletin of the American Schools of Oriental Research*, No. 89 (February, 1943), pp. 29-32.
—, Review of *Introduction to the Old Testament*, by Robert H. Pfeiffer, *Journal of Biblical Literature*, Vol. LXI (June, 1942), pp. 111-26.
—, "The Role of the Canaanites in the History of Civilization", *The Bible and the Ancient Near East*, ed. G. Ernest Wright (Garden City, N.J.: Doubleday & Co. Inc., 1961), pp. 328-62.
—, "Some Canaanite-Phoenician Sources of Hebrew Wisdom", *Wisdom in Israel and in the Ancient Near East,* eds. H.H. Rowley, Martin Noth, D. Winton Thomas (= Supplements to *Vetus Testamentum*, Vol. III) (Leiden: E.J. Brill, 1960, pp. 1-15).
—, "A Teacher to a Man of Shechem About 1400 B.C.", *Bulletin of the American Schools of Oriental Research*, No. 86 (April, 1942), pp. 28-31.
Anderson, Robert T., "Was Isaiah a Scribe?"*Journal of Biblical Literature*, Vol. LXXIX (March, 1960), pp. 57-58.
Baab, Otto J., "The Book of Job", *Interpretation*, Vol. V (July, 1951), pp. 329-43.
Baumgartner, Walter, "Die israelitische Weisheitliteratur", *Theologische Rundschau*, Vol. V (1933), pp. 259-88.
—, "The Wisdom Literature", *The Old Testament and Modern Study*, ed. H.H. Rowley (Oxford: At the Clarendon Press, 1951), pp. 210-37.
Beecher, W.J., "The Wisdom Literature", *The Bible as Literature*, by Richard Green Moulton, *et al.* 6th ed. (New York: Thomas Y. Crowell & Co., 1896), pp. 105-21.
Black, Matthew, "Scribe", *The Interpreter's Dictionary of the Bible*, eds. George Arthur Buttrick *et al.*, Vol. IV, pp. 246-48.
Blank, Sheldon H., "Proverb", *The Interpreter's Dictionary of the Bible*, eds. George Arthur Buttrick *et al.*, Vol. III, pp. 934-36.
Boas, Franz, "Literature, Music, and Dance", *General Anthropology*, ed. Franz Boas (New York: D.C. Heath & Co., 1938), pp. 589-608.
Boer, P.A.H. de, "The Counsellor", *Wisdom in Israel and in the Ancient Near East*, eds. H.H. Rowley, Martin Noth, D. Winton Thomas (= Supplements to *Vetus Testamentum*, Vol. III) (Leiden: E.J. Brill, 1960), pp. 42-71.
Boston, James R., "The Wisdom Influence Upon the Song of Moses", *Journal of Biblical Literature*, Vol. LXXXVII (June, 1968), pp. 198-202.
Brunner, Hellmut, "Die Weisheitsliteratur", *Handbuch der Orientalistik*, Part I, No. 1 (Leiden: E.J. Brill, 1952), pp. 90-110.
Buzy, D., "Les Machals numérique de la sangsue et de l'almah (Prov. XXX 15-16.18-20)", *Revue Biblique*, Vol. XLII (1933), pp. 5-13.

Carmichael, C.M., "Deuteronomic Laws, Wisdom, and Historical Traditions", *Journal of Semitic Studies*, Vol. XII (1967), pp. 198-206.

Causse, A., "Introduction à l'étude de la sagesse juive", *Revue d'histoire et de Philosophie religieuses*, Vol. I (1921), pp. 45-60.

—, "Sagesse égyptienne et sagesse juive", *Revue d'histoire et de Philosophie religieuses*, Vol. IX (March-April, 1929), pp. 149-69.

Cazelles, H., "A Propos d'une Phrase de H.H. Rowley", *Wisdom in Israel and in the Ancient Near East*, eds. H.H. Rowley, Martin Noth, D. Winton Thomas (= Supplements to *Vetus Testamentum*, Vol. III) (Leiden: E.J. Brill, 1960), pp. 26-31.

Conrad, J., "Die innere Gleiderung der Proverbien; Zur Frage nach der Systematisierung des Spruchgutes in den älteren Teilsammlungen", *Zeitschrift für die alttestamentliche Wissenschaft*, Vol. LXXIX (1967), pp. 67-76.

Crenshaw, J.L., "The Influence of the Wise Upon Amos; the Doxologies of Amos and Job 5:9-16, 9:5-10", *Zeitschrift für die alttestamentliche Wissenschaft*, Vol. LXXIX (1967), pp. 42-52.

—, "Method in Determining Wisdom Influence Upon 'Historical' Literature", *Journal of Biblical Literature*, Vol. LXXXVIII (June, 1969), pp. 129-42.

Driver, Godfrey Rolles, Review of *Before the Bible*, by Cyrus H. Gordon, *Journal of Semitic Studies*, Vol. VIII (Autumn, 1963), pp. 277-81.

Drubbel, Adrien, "Le Conflit entre la sagesse profane et la sagesse réligieuse", *Biblica* (1936), pp. 407-28.

Dunsmore, Marion Hiller, "An Egyptian Contribution to the Book of Proverbs", *The Journal of Religion*, Vol. V (May, 1925), pp. 300-08.

Eichrodt, Walther, "Vorsehungsglaube und Theodizee im Alten Testament", *Festschrift Otto Procksch* (Leipzig: A. Deichert), pp. 45-70.

Eissfeldt, Otto, "The Literature of Israel: Modern Criticism", *Record and Revelation*, ed. H. Wheeler Robinson (Oxford: At the Clarendon Press, 1938), pp. 74-109.

Elmslie, W.A.L., "The Religion of Israel: Ethics", *Record and Revelation*, ed. H. Wheeler Robinson (Oxford: At the Clarendon Press, 1938), pp. 275-302.

Feinberg, C.L., "The Poetic Structure of the Book of Job and the Ugaritic Literature", *Bibliotheca Sacra*, Vol. CIII (1946), pp. 283-92.

Fensham, F. Charles, "Widow, Orphan, and the Poor in Ancient Near Eastern Legal and Wisdom Literature", *Journal of Near Eastern Studies*, Vol. XXI (January-October, 1962), pp. 129-39.

Fichtner, Johannes, "Jesaja unter den Weisen", *Theologische Literaturzeitung*, Vol. LXXIV (February, 1949), cols. 75-80.

Fine, Hillel A., "The Tradition of a Patient Job", *Journal of Biblical Literature*, Vol. LXXIV (March, 1955), pp. 28-32.

Fohrer, Georg, "Überlieferung und Wandlung der Hioblegend", *Festschrift Friedrich Baumgärtel* (*Erlanger Forschungen*, Reihe A: *Geisteswissenschaften*, Vol. 10) (Erlangen: Für den Druck herausgegeben von Leonhard Rost, 1959), pp. 41-62.

Forman, Charles C., "The Context of Biblical Wisdom", *Hibbert Journal*, Vol. LX (January, 1962), pp. 125-32.

Fortes, Meyer, "Mind", *The Institutions of Primitive Society* (Glencoe, Illinois: The Free Press, 1956), pp. 81-94.

Fosbroke, E.W., "The Book of Amos, Introduction and Exegesis", *The Interpreter's Bible*, Vol. VI, pp. 763-853.

Fox, Michael V., "Aspects of the Religion of the Book of Proverbs", *Hebrew Union College Annual*, Vol. XXXIX (1968), pp. 55-69.

Frankfort, H. and H.A. Frankfort, "The Emancipation of Thought from Myth", *The Intellectual Adventure of Ancient Man*, by H. Frankfort *et al.* (Chicago: The University of Chicago Press, 1946), pp. 363-88.

Fritsch, Charles T., "The Book of Proverbs, Introduction and Exegesis", *The Interpreter's Bible*, Vol. IV, pp. 765-957.

—, "The Gospel in the Book of Proverbs", *Theology Today*, Vol. VII (April, 1950), pp. 169-83.

Genung, J.F., "The Development of Hebrew Wisdom", *The Biblical World*, Vol. XLII (July-December, 1913), pp. 16-25.

Gerstenberger, Erhard, "Covenant and Commandment", *Journal of Biblical Literature*, Vol. LXXXIV (March, 1965), pp. 38-51.

Ginsberg, H.L., "The Structure and Contents of the Book of Koheleth", *Wisdom in Israel and in the Ancient near East*, eds. H.H. Rowley, Martin Noth, D. Winton Thomas (= Supplements to *Vetus Testamentum*, Vol. III) (Leiden: E.J. Brill, 1960), pp. 138-49.

Godbey, Allan Howard, "The Hebrew *Mašal*", *American Journal of Semitic Languages and Literatures*, Vol. XXXIX (January, 1923), pp. 89-108.

Gordis, Robert, "The Social Background of Wisdom Literature", *Hebrew Union College Annual*, Vol. XVIII (1943-44), pp. 77-118.

Gordon, Cyrus H., "Homer and Bible", *Hebrew Union College Annual*, Vol. XXVI (1955), pp. 43-108.

Gordon, Edmund I., "The Sumerian Proverb Collection: A Preliminary Report", *Journal of the American Oriental Society*, Vol. LXXIV (April-June, 1954), pp. 82-85.

—, "Sumerian Proverbs: 'Collection Four' ", *Journal of the American Oriental Society*, Vol. LXXVII (April-June, 1957), pp. 67-79.

Gottwald, Norman K., "Poetry, Hebrew", *The Interpreter's Dictionary of the Bible*, eds. George Arthur Buttrick *et. al.*, Vol. III, pp. 829-38.

Gressmann, Hugo, "Die neugefundene Lehre des Amen-em-ope und die vorexilische Spruchdichtung Israels", *Zeitschrift für die alttestamentliche Wissenschaft*, Vol. XLII (1924), pp. 272-96.

Griffith, Francis L., "The Teaching of Amenophis, the Son of Kanekht", *Journal of Egyptian Archeology*, Vol. XII (1926), pp. 191-231.

Harrelson, Walter J., "Wisdom and Pastoral Theology", *Andover Newton Quarterly*, Vol. VII (September, 1966), pp. 6-14.

Hempel, Johannes, "The Forms of Oral Tradition", *Record and Revelation*, ed. H. Wheeler Robinson (Oxford: At the Clarendon Press, 1938), pp. 28-44.

—, "Das theologische Problem des Hiob", *Zeitschrift für systematische Theologie*, Vol. VI (1929), pp. 621-89.

Heseltine, Janet E., "Introduction", *The Oxford Dictionary of English Proverbs with Introduction and Index by Janet E. Heseltine*, ed. George William Smith (Oxford: At the Clarendon Press, 1935), pp. vii-xxvii.

Holladay, W.L., "Isa. III 10-11: An Archaic Wisdom Passage", *Vetus Testamentum*, Vol. XVIII (October, 1968), pp. 481-87.

Humbert, Paul, "Le Modernisme de Job", *Wisdom in Israel and in the Ancient Near East*, eds. H.H. Rowley, Martin Noth, D. Winton Thomas (= Supplements to *Vetus Testamentum*, Vol. III) (Leiden: E.J. Brill, 1960), pp. 162-69.

Irwin, William A., "The Hebrews", *The Intellectual Adventure of Ancient Man*, by H. Frankfort, *et al.* (Chicago: The University of Chicago Press, 1946), pp. 223-360.

—, "Job", *Peake's Commentary on the Bible*, eds. Matthew Black and H.H. Rowley (New York: Thomas Nelson and Sons Ltd., 1962), pp. 391-408.

—, "The Wisdom Literature", *The Interpreter's Bible*, Vol. I, pp. 212-19.

James, Fleming, "Some Aspects of the Religion of Proverbs", *Journal of Biblical Literature*, Vol. LI, Part 1 (1932), p. 31-39.

Johnson, A.R., "מָשָׁל", *Wisdom in Israel and in the Ancient Near East*, eds. H.H. Rowley, Martin Noth, D. Winton Thomas (= Supplements to *Vetus Testamentum*, Vol. III) (Leiden: E.J. Brill, 1960), pp. 162-69.

Keimer, Ludwig L., "The Wisdom of Amenemope and the Proverbs of Solomon", *American Journal of Semitic Languages and Literatures*, Vol. XLIII (1926-27), pp. 8-21.

Kimble, George H.T., "Words to the Wise – From Africa", The *New York Times Magazine* (January 28, 1962), p. 51.

König, Eduard, "Parable (in OT)", *A Dictionary of the Bible*, ed. James Hastings (New York: Charles Scribner's Sons, 1901), pp. 660-62.

Kramer, Samuel Noah, " 'Man and His God': A Sumerian Variation on the 'Job' Motif", *Wisdom in Israel and in the Ancient Near East*, eds. H.H. Rowley, Martin Noth, D. Winton Thomas (= Supplements to *Vetus Testamentum*, Vol. III) (Leiden: E.J. Brill, 1960), pp. 170-82.

—, "Sumerian Wisdom Literature: A Preliminary Survey", *Bulletin of the American Schools of Oriental Research*, No. 122 (April, 1951), pp. 28-31.

Langdon, Stephen, "Babylonian Proverbs", *American Journal of Semitic Languages and Literatures*, Vol. XXVIII (July, 1912), pp. 217-43.

Lauha, Aarre, "Die Krise des Religiösen Glaubens bei Kohelet", *Wisdom in Israel and in the Ancient Near East*, eds. H.H. Rowley, Martin Noth, D. Winton Thomas (= Supplements to *Vetus Testamentum*, Vol. III) (Leiden: E.J. Brill, 1960), pp. 183-91.

Lexa, F., "Dieu et Dieux dans l'enseignement d'Amenemopet", *Archiv Orientální*, Vol. I (1929), pp. 163-70.

Lienhardt, Godfrey, "Modes of Thought", *The Institutions of Primitive Society* (Glencoe, Illinois: The Free Press, 1956), pp. 95-107.

Lindblom, Johannes, "Wisdom in the Old Testament Prophets", *Wisdom in Israel and in the Ancient Near East*, eds. H.H. Rowley, Martin Noth, D. Winton Thomas (= Supplements to *Vetus Testamentum*, Vol. III) (Leiden: E.J. Brill, 1960), pp. 192-204.

Little, Kenneth, "The Mende in Sierre Leone", *African Worlds*, ed. Daryll Forde (London: Oxford University Press), pp. 111-37.

Lods, Adolphe, "Recherches récentes sur le livre de Job", *Revue D'Histoire et de Philosophie religieuses*, Vol. XIV (1934), pp. 501-33.

Loeb, Edwin M., "The Function of Proverbs in the Intellectual Development of Primitive Peoples", *The Scientific Monthly*, Vol. LXXIV (February, 1952), pp. 100-04.

—, "Kuanyama Ambo Folklore", *Anthropological Records,* Vol. XIII (Berkeley: University of California Press, 1951), pp. 289-335.

McKenzie, John L., "Reflections on Wisdom", *Journal of Biblical Literature*, Vol. LXXXVI (March, 1967), pp. 1-9.

Malfroy, Jean, "Sagesse et Loi dans le Deutéronome", *Vetus Testamentum*, Vol. XV (January, 1965), pp. 49-65.

Mays, James L., Review of *Wesen und Geschichte der Weisheit* by Hans Heinrich Schmid, *Interpretation*, Vol. XXIII (July, 1969), pp. 344-46.

Mendenhall, George D. "Ancient Oriental and Biblical Law", *The Biblical Archeologist*, Vol. XVII (May, 1954), pp. 26-46.

—, "Covenant Forms in Israelite Tradition", *The Biblical Archeologist*, Vol. XVII (September, 1954), pp. 50-76.

Mercer, Samuel A.B., "The Wisdom of Amenemope and his Religious Ideas", *Egyptian Religion*, Vol. II (April, 1934), pp. 27-69.

Messenger, J.C., "Anang Proverb-Riddles", *Journal of American Folklore*, Vol. LXXIII (July, 1960), pp. 225-35.

—, "The Role of Proverbs in a Nigerian Judicial System", *Southwestern Journal of Anthropology*, Vol. XV (Spring, 1959), pp. 64-73.

Morgenstern, Julian, "Universalism and Particularism", *The Universal Jewish Encyclopedia*, Vol. X, pp. 353-57.

Mowinckel, Sigmund, "Psalms and Wisdom", *Wisdom in Israel and in the Ancient Near East*, eds. H.H. Rowley, Martin Noth, D. Winton Thomas (= Supplements to *Vetus Testamentum*, Vol. III) (Leiden: E.J. Brill, 1960), pp. 205-24.

Murphy, Roland E., "Assumptions and Problems in Old Testament Wisdom Research", *Catholic Biblical Quarterly*, Vol. XXIX (July, 1967), pp. 101-12.

—, "A Consideration of the Classification 'Wisdom Psalms' ", *Congress Volume, Bonn 1962,* ed. P.A.H. De Boer (= Supplements to *Vetus Testamentum*, Vol. IX) (Leiden: E.J. Brill, 1963), pp. 156-67.

—, "Form Criticism and Wisdom Literature ", *Catholic Biblical Quarterly*, Vol. XXXI (October, 1969), pp. 475-83.

—, "The Interpretation of Old Testament Wisdom Literature", *Interpretation*, Vol. XXIII (July, 1969), pp. 289-301.

—, "The Kerygma of the Book of Proverbs", *Interpretation*, Vol. XX (January, 1966), pp. 3-14.

Nougayrol, Jean, "Une version ancienne du 'Juste souffrant' ", *Revue Biblique*, Vol. LIX (1952), pp. 239-50.

Oesterley, William O.E., "The Teaching of Amen-em-ope and the Old Testament", *Zeitschrift für die alttestamentliche Wissenschaft*, Vol. XLV (1927), pp. 9-24.

Pederson, Johannes, "Scepticisme israélite", *Revue d'Histoire et de Philosophie religieuses*, Vol. X (July-October 1930), pp. 317-70.

Pei, Mario, "Parallel Proverbs", *Saturday Review* (May 2, 1964), pp. 16-17, 53.

Pfeiffer, Robert H., "Wisdom and Vision in the Old Testament", *Zeitschrift für die alttestamenliche Wissenschaft*, Vol. LII (1934), pp. 93-101.

Pope, Marvin H., "Job, Book of", *The Interpreter's Dictionary of the Bible*, eds. George Arthur Buttrick *et al.*, Vol. II, pp. 911-25.

—, Review of *Before the Bible* by Cyrus Gordon, *Journal of Biblical Literature*, Vol. LXXXIII (March, 1964), pp. 72-76.

Porteous, Norman W., "The Basis of the Ethical Teaching of the Prophets", *Studies in Old Testament Prophecy*, ed. H.H. Rowley (Edinburgh: T. & T. Clark, 1946), pp. 143-56.

—, "Royal Wisdom", *Wisdom in Israel and in the Ancient Near East*, eds. H.H. Rowley, Martin Noth, D. Winton Thomas (= Supplements to *Vetus Testamentum*, Vol. III) (Leiden: E.J. Brill, 1960), pp. 247-61.

—, "The Theology of the Old Testament", *Peake's Commentary on the Bible*, eds. Matthew Black and H.H. Rowley (New York: Thomas Nelson and Sons Ltd., 1962), pp. 151-59.

Priest, John F., "Where is Wisdom to be Placed?" *The Journal of Bible and Religion*, Vol. XXXI (October, 1963), pp. 275-82.

Rad, Gerhard von, "Aspekte alttestamentlichen Weltverständnisses", *Evangelische Theologie*, Vol. XXIV (February, 1964), pp. 57-73.

—, "Das theologische Problem des alttestamenlichen Schöpfungsglaubens", *Werden und Wesen des A.T. (Beihefte zur Zeitschrift für die alttestamentliche Wissenschaft*, Vol. LXVI) (1946), pp. 138-47.

Rankin, O.S., "The Book of Ecclesiastes, Introduction and Exegesis", *The Interpreter's Bible*, Vol. V, pp. 3-88.

Reichard, Gladys A., "Social Life", *General Anthropology*, ed. Franz Boas (New York: D.C. Heath & Co., 1938), pp. 409-86.

Robert, A., ,"Le Yahwisme de Prov. X,1-XXII,16; XXV-XXIX", *Memorial Lagrange*, eds. J. Gabalda *et al.* (Paris: Librairie Lecoffre, 1940), pp. 163-82.

Robinson, H. Wheeler, "The Theology of the Old Testament", *Record and Revelation*, ed. H. Wheeler Robinson (Oxford: At the Clarendon Press, 1938), pp. 303-48.

Rowley, H.H., "Moses and the Decalogue", *Bulletin of the John Rylands Library*, Vol. XXXIV (1951), pp. 81-118.

Ryder, E.T., "Ecclesiastes", *Peake's Commentary on the Bible*, eds. Matthew Black and H.H. Rowley (New York: Thomas Nelson and Sons Ltd., 1962), pp. 458-67.

—, "Form Criticism of the Old Testament", *Peake's Commentary on the Bible*, eds. Matthew Black and H.H. Rowley (New York: Thomas Nelson and Sons Ltd., 1962), pp. 91-95.

Rylaarsdam, J. Coert, "The Proverbs", *Peake's Commentary on the Bible*, eds. Matthew Black and H.H. Rowley (New York: Thomas Nelson and Sons Ltd., 1962), pp. 444-57.

Sarna, Nahum, "Epic Substratum in the Prose of Job", *Journal of Biblical Literature*, Vol. LXXVI (March, 1957), pp. 13-25.

Scott, R.B.Y., "Priesthood, Prophecy, Wisdom, and the Knowledge of God", *Journal of Biblical Literature*, Vol. LXXX (March 1961), p. 1-15.

—, "Solomon and the Beginning of Wisdom in Israel", *Wisdom in Israel and in the Ancient Near East*, eds. H.H. Rowley, Martin Noth, D. Winton Thomas (= Supplements to *Vetus Testamentum*, Vol. III) (Leiden: E.J. Brill, 1960), pp. 262-79.

Simpson, D.C., "The Hebrew Book of Proverbs and the Teaching of Ameno-phis", *Journal of Egyptain Archeology*, Vol. XII (1926), pp. 232-39.

Smith, George Adam, "The Hebrew Genius as Exhibited in the Old Testament", *The Legacy of Israel*, eds. Edwyn R. Bevan and Charles Singer (Oxford: At the Clarendon Press, 1927).

Speiser, E.A., "Ancient Mesopotamia", *The Idea of History in the Ancient Near East*, ed. Robert C. Dentan (=*American Oriental Series*, Vol. XXXVIII) (New Haven: Yale University Press, 1955), pp. 35-76.

Story, Cullen I.K., "The Book of Proverbs and Northwest-Semitic Literature", *Journal of Biblical Literature*, Vol. LXIV September, 1945), pp. 319-37.

Terrien, Samuel, "Amos and Wisdom", *Israel's Prophetic Heritage*, eds. Bernard W. Anderson and Walter Harrelson (New York: Harper & Brothers, 1962), pp. 108-115.

—, "The Book of Job, Introduction and Exegesis", *The Interpreter's Bible*, Vol. III, pp. 877-1198.

Toombs, Lawrence E., "Old Testament Theology and the Wisdom Literature", *Journal of Bible and Religion*, Vol. XXIII (July, 1955), pp. 193-96.

Weinfeld, M., "The Origin of the Humanism in Deuteronomy", *Journal of Biblical Literature*, Vol. LXXX (September, 1961), pp. 241-47.

Williams, Ronald J., "Theodicy in the Ancient Near East", *Canadian Journal of Theology*, Vol. II (January, 1956), pp. 14-26.

Wilson, John A., "Egypt: The Nature of the Universe", *The Intellectual Adventure of Ancient Man*, by H. Frankfort *et al.* (Chicago: The University of Chicago Press, 1946), pp. 31-36.

Wolf, C.U., "Recorder", *The Interpreter's Dictionary of the Bible*, eds. George Arthur Buttrick *et al.*, Vol. IV, p. 18.

Zimmerli, Walther, "The Place and Limit of the Wisdom in the Framework of the Old Testament Theology", *Scottish Journal of Theology*, Vol. XVII (June, 1964), pp. 146-58.

—, "Zur Struktur der alttestamentliche Weisheit", *Zeitschrift für die alttestamentliche Wissenschaft*, Vol. LI (1933), pp. 177-204.

OTHER SOURCES

Clasper, Paul, Personal interview (March 2, 1964).

INDEX